God Is Love

"For God so loved the world that he gave his only begotten Son, that whosoever believeth in him should not perish, but have everlasting life."

—John 3:16

G. E. FIFIELD

Originally published by
Theodore Reese
156 LaSalle Street
Chicago, Illinois

Republished by
HeavenlySanctuary.com
Redlands, California

Republished 2008 by HeavenlySanctuary.com
Printed in the United States of America

Edited by Dorothee Cole
Page design by Page One Communications
Cover design by Lars Justinen
Illustration of hands by Darrel Tank/GoodSalt.com

This republished book has been electronically scanned from the original. Therefore, grammar, punctuation, spelling, and other style elements will reflect the prevailing usage of the late nineteenth century.

ISBN: 978-0-9815942-0-0

Contents

Dedication

To the friends whose love and trust have gladdened and glorified his days; and to the many kindred hearts, who, though yet unknown, are still, through kindred experiences, being led along the converging paths that center at the throne, to blend their lives forever in the glory and joy of immortal friendship, this little book is affectionately dedicated by the Author.

—January 1, 1897

Preface

God is Love. There is, indeed, no greater knowledge, no greater source of healing than what is contained in these three words. Yet Timothy tells us that no one has ever seen God and no one can ever see Him (1 Timothy 6:16). If this is true, how can we humans ever truly know and trust God?

The boundless Creator of the universe, infinite in power and knowledge, condescended into the womb of one of his own creatures, lived the life of a servant, and died the death of a criminal. But how is this love, you may ask? *God became a human being,* so that we could see and understand His character, trust His Person, and learn to love and appreciate His ways and eventually be healed from all our brokenness through the power of His unspeakable love.

The publishers believe that this modest volume, originally published in 1897 and virtually hidden away for over a century, *uniquely* expresses the unsurpassable love of our Heavenly Father with such clarity and truth, that its re-publication seemed an absolute necessity. Two thousand years after the life and death of Jesus, far too many are still afraid of God, shackled with the belief that God needs to be appeased and that He requires blood in order to forgive us. The pagan belief that Jesus died to create love for us in the heart of the Father and to shield us from His wrath, is beautifully replaced by the Good News that Jesus came to reveal the Father's heart of love, so that the Father might hold us tightly in His arms of love.

No truth is as paramount in significance as the truth about the character of God Almighty. *This* is the truth that has the power to set free imprisoned hearts and minds to a living faith that God is indeed Love personified. We humbly submit that *this* is the sole intent of our efforts to re-publish Fifield's work.

For His glory alone,

The Publishers

Author's Preface

These chapters first appeared some four years since, published as a serial in one of our weekly religious journals. Since that time, the writer has never ceased to receive requests that they be put in some more permanent form. This little book is the result. The author is very sensible of its imperfections and limitations.

Of the many subjects touched, not one is treated exhaustively, but all are only used for the moment, as God uses the sunset clouds, or the snow on the mountain's summit, merely to reflect to darkened eyes, low down in the valley, the glory of his goodness.

Born of the heart, it is humbly hoped these words may speak to the heart; and that some poor souls, driven by doubt and wandering wearily because of sin, may behold here revealed the mystic ladder leading from the Bethel stone of their present hunger and loneliness to the light and warmth and plenty of the Father's House.

—G. E. F.

Acknowledgments

The Publishers want to express their gratitude for the individuals without whom the publication of this book would not have been possible. We'd like to thank Tom Ewall for originally making us aware of "God is Love". We are grateful to Jim Baden for providing us with the scanned original text by G.E. Fifield, so that it could be converted into word processor text via optical character recognition (OCR) software. We are indebted to Brent Hildebrand, M.D. who, with the help of unnamed others, created a faithful reproduction of the original text by comparing the OCR copy and an independently typed copy which aided greatly in the elimination of any errors. Last, but definitely not least, we are grateful to Dorothy Hildebrand, Ed.D. and Tom Ewall for their invaluable amount of time typing, reading and comparing the text, as well as to all the members of the HeavenlySanctuary.com team, who made this project possible.

"Greater love hath no man than this, that a man lay down his life for his friends."

—Jesus

1

Knowing God

"He that loveth not knoweth not God, for God is love."
—1 John 4:8

"God is love." These three words of only nine letters contain a revelation of God greater than men or angels will ever be able fully to fathom. In fact, to know more of their meaning, to be constantly learning more of their meaning, will be the work and the wisdom, the pleasure and the poetry, of the redeemed throughout eternity. To comprehend the meaning of these words is to know God and Jesus Christ, and to know these is life eternal.[1] In truth, there is no knowledge outside of them; for in them are hid all the treasures of wisdom and knowledge, and without is only ignorance and darkness.[2]

This is no figure of speech, it is the simple statement of a fact. To say that any man has had a thought of truth or an item of knowledge that God did not have before him, is to say that in that respect the man is in advance of his Maker; and that would be to deny the omniscience of God. Although they cannot lead to wicked actions in him as they do in us, yet even our wicked thoughts are known to God before we think them. The psalmist says: "O Lord, thou hast searched me, and known me. Thou knowest my downsitting and mine uprising, *thou understandest my thought afar off.*"[3] And Job answered the Lord and said, "I know that thou canst do everything, and that no thought can be withholden from thee."[4] David is yet more bold, for he says, "The Lord searcheth *all hearts* and understandeth all *the imaginations* of the *thoughts.*"

No wonder that grand old Kepler, as he gazed into the heavens, computing and measuring the motions of the planets, till, one after another, the sublime laws of planetary motion burst upon his bewildered mind,—no wonder that, with brimming eyes and throbbing heart, he exclaimed, "O God, I think thy thoughts after thee!" The best that any astronomer can do is to think reverently God's thoughts after him, and perchance trace the working out of some of those thoughts through the wondrous star-gemmed pathways of the sky. All the student of zoology can do is to trace the thoughts of God through the varied forms of animal life, discovering at every step the evidences of the infinite Mind that has preceded him.

The botanist traces the same Mind through the orders and families of the vegetable kingdom, finding in every leaf and every flower an infinity of beauty revealed, which, even with the aid of all his microscopes, he cannot comprehend; and yet he knows and feels that the infinite Mind has thought it all out before him, and that every thought was a thought of love. The very buds on the trees grow in accordance with a mathematical law, and he sees that God had numbered them all before they came.

Faith sees but a short step from all this to the truth that Jesus taught when he said: "The very hairs of your head are all numbered. Fear ye not, therefore." What wonder that David said: "Thou, Lord, hast made me glad through thy work; I will triumph in the works of thy hands. O Lord, how great are thy works! and thy thoughts are very deep." From the mightiest sun that swings in space to the smallest flower blooming at my feet, there is an infinity in everything; and if we read aright, we soon discover it to be an infinity of all-comprehending and all-encompassing love, for God is love. Thus we think God's thoughts after him, till our own hearts are filled with love ineffable.

The poet's soul never thrilled with a pure emotion but he caught the thought from God, revealed somewhere in his work or his word. The mighty harmony whose first full pulse almost burst the enraptured musician's heart, descended through dim distances from the angel choir; his sensitive ear only caught and reproduced it here. So all study is the study of God, all knowledge is included in knowing him, and to know him is to know love, for "God is love."

The visitor in Washington, looking from the dome of the capitol, discovers that all streets lead toward him. The capitol is the hub from which all the streets radiate to the city and to the nation. In the great empire of Rome, it was said all roads led to Rome. So God sits in the center of his mighty universe, and every path of knowledge is a magnificent avenue leading to his throne, an avenue on which he who walks does well to pause, and wonder, and worship at every object passed, even as the ancient traveler at the wayside shrine, wondering and worshiping, seeing God in everything, only taking care to keep his face onward toward the throne and to be prepared for greater glory farther on.

The pantheist and the agnostic champion of a science falsely so called, may walk backward admiring the pebbles by the way, and persistently refuse to see anything but what they have already passed; but faith chooses rather to leave those things which are behind, and press forward to those things which are before, beholding each new object, and the whole avenue before, in the magnificent light of the throne. "To such a one," Carlisle well says, "the universe is not a kitchen and a cattle stall merely, but an oracle and a temple as well." For him the mystery does not vanish with the superficial explanations of science, but through these he sees all mysteries broadening and deepening, and resolving themselves into the one great sweet, mystery of God,—and God is love. It is not strange that this should be so. It is like God, a God who would lead all men to him, if only they would be led.

We see the same thing in his word as in his work. The first commandment includes the whole decalogue; the message of the first angel of Revelation 14 includes all three messages; the first sermon of Christ includes the whole gospel. Why? Because God would arrange it so that the logical mind, receiving the first glimmerings of truth, might be led thereby step by step into the whole truth, and to himself the God of truth. This is because God is love. Even so in his work: if we but trace his thought, we shall find from the smallest insect, studied only under the most powerful magnifying glass, up to the largest suns and worlds, stepping-stones upward, yea, a magnificent stairway leading to him.

This is what Paul meant when he says: "The invisible things of him from the creation of the world are clearly seen, being understood by the things that are made, even his eternal power and Godhead; so that they [the heathen] are without excuse." And David tells the same truth: "The heavens declare the glory of God, and the firmament showeth his handiwork. Day unto day uttereth speech, and night unto night showeth knowledge. There is no speech nor language, where their voice is not heard."[5] All knowledge is in him, so night unto night reveals him. His glory is his goodness. So the heavens declare his goodness; and for him who has eyes to see, and ears to hear, and a heart to understand, the heavens and earth, day and night, unite in varied harmonious voices, to proclaim in every land and every tongue that God is love.

Notes:

1. John 17:3.
2. Col. 2:3.
3. Ps. 139:1, 2.
4. Job. 42:2.
5. Ps. 19:1–3.

II

The Attributes of God

"I know not where his islands lift
Their fronded palms in air,
I only know I cannot drift
Beyond his love and care."

—Whittier

"God is love." The study of these words is the study of a God in whom are hid all the treasures of wisdom and knowledge. God has revealed himself both in his work and in his word, and these revelations agree in this truth. All that the broadest science can do is to comprehend something of the plan of creation, and this whole creation is but the materialization of the divine thought. The plan is God's—a part of the infinite Mind.

What the word of God seeks to do is to reveal in human language the divine plan of redemption, a plan disclosing such infinite depths of love that even the angels desire to look into it. Even they who constantly dwell in the full light of that love, unclouded by sin or sorrow—even they behold here unknown expanses and unfathomed depths; and if asked what they most thought revealed the love of God for his creatures, they would undoubtedly answer, "God so loved the world, that he gave his only begotten Son, that whosoever believeth in him should not perish, but have everlasting life."

"God is love." What do the words mean? What can they mean but that love is the controlling characteristic in the mind of God, the one attribute of Deity from which all other attributes spring, and back into which they can all be traced? The Scriptures do not say that God is power; they say he is powerful, almighty. We see his power manifested in creating and upholding the universe; but his power separated from his love would but reveal to him our weakness until we became contemptible in his sight. The two must not be separated.

What the soul, wearied with its own hopeless struggle against sin, needs to see, is not that he is less powerful, but that *his power is his love.* What is the moral power of the universe but the power of love? Said Napoleon, while languishing in exile on the barren rock of St. Helena, "Alexander, Julius Caesar, and myself founded kingdoms by the power of our arms, and today who cares for us? But Jesus Christ founded a kingdom by the *power of his love,* and today millions would die for him."

Satan has no power to force a man arbitrarily to do wrong. If he did have that power, the wrong would be solely in him, and not in the man thus forced. All evil, as all good, lies in the mind that directs the action. If by taking hold of one who is weaker than I am, I force him to thrust a dagger into his neighbor, it was my mind, not his, that directed the blow, and in me solely lies the sin. If he consents to my act, he becomes partner in the guilt. If I could force his mind on every subject by thus putting my mind in the place of his own, he would cease to have any separate existence from me, and hence would have no character, either good or bad. So God cannot force the mind arbitrarily to dictate good actions. To do that would be to destroy individual identity, and make all men but machines to manifest God's mind.

The power of Satan is therefore solely the power to *lead men* who submit their minds to him, into evil. And the power of God to redeem the world is solely the power of his love to lead men who submit their minds to him, into righteousness. God's power is therefore his love. Nor can this be limited to mere moral power. What is the power that created and that upholds the universe? Agnostic science may prate learnedly of evolution and gravitation, but faith sees the same infinite Love, without whom not a sparrow falleth to the ground, creating and upholding suns and worlds, that there may be light, and heat, and home for all his creatures. Thus the power of God is his love, and why need we fear? Perfect love casteth out fear by revealing the fact that the infinite reservoir of almighty force is held at the dictation of that love that gathereth the lambs in his arms, and tenderly carrieth them in his bosom.

And what about the wisdom of God? We see his wonderful wisdom revealed in the harmonious revolution of the planets in their orbits, each with clocklike precision completing its revolution at just the right time, though hundreds of years in making it; all crossing and recrossing one another's paths in the heavens, yet never dashing into each other. This reveals his wisdom, and also his love for his creatures, if we look with other than blind eyes. His wisdom separated from his love would but teach him our weakness and foolishness.

Shut in behind the impenetrable future, and peering with but faulty vision into the poorly comprehended past, what the soul, thus painfully conscious of its own limitations, wants to know is that God's wisdom is his love, and that all the future, to it so dark, is held in Love's hands.

After all, what is the world's foolishness but its rebellion against the wisdom of God's law, which is love?—a rebellion and a foolishness which have given birth to every throb of human pain and every wail of human anguish. Eternity will demonstrate that the wisdom of God was but the wisdom of a fatherly, solicitous love, that saw the inevitable end of each course of action from the beginning, and only forbade those things which would lead to misery.

And what is justice, the justice of God, but another name for his love? Our partial love may make us unjust. If I love A more than B, I may be unjust to B, but this injustice is not the result of my love for A, but rather of the imperfection of my love in its lack toward B. The moment we conceive of a love that is infinite and all-embracing, that moment we see that that love includes justice. Can he who loves all his children be unjust to any of them? Thus justice is love, and he, the dread One, holding the balances in his hands, is he beyond whose love and care we cannot stray, though we may often grieve his Spirit.

And what shall I say of the wrath of God, spoken of so many times in the Scripture? Jesus Christ came to reveal the Father. There never was a being on this earth who loved the sinner as did he, and never one who so perfectly and completely hated the sin. His love for the sinner was as infinite as his hatred for the sin. In him is revealed a God who ever and always completely separates between the sinner and the sin. He hates the sin, because it is the enemy of the sinner, whom he loves. If I have a friend, and know of an assassin who is lurking for his life, the measure of my love for that friend is the measure of my hatred for that assassin.

Sin is the only enemy of the human race. It lurks insidiously behind ten thousand beautiful forms of pleasure, and ever lurks with murderous intent. All God's hatred is his hatred for sin. All his wrath is his wrath against sin. This hatred and wrath are simply his love for the sinner, whom sin is seeking to destroy. The plan of redemption is God's effort, by revealing his infinite love, to separate the sin from the sinner, so that sin may be destroyed, misery banished, and the universe clean, and yet the sinner saved.

Only those who finally and inseparably connect themselves with sin, so that God cannot destroy the one without destroying the other, will have to drink God's wrath against sin. Love takes no pleasure in this even. "As I live, saith the Lord God, I have no pleasure in the death of the wicked; but that the wicked turn from his way and live; turn ye, turn ye from your evil ways; for why will ye die?"

Thus all the attributes of God are traced back to the one attribute, and "God is love." "Love is of God; and every one that loveth is born of God, and knoweth God. He that loveth not knoweth not God, for God is love." There is nothing in God but love, for love includes everything good. His love reaches to the outermost rim of his mighty universe, and takes in its constant care all his creatures, never leaving them for a moment, however much they may grieve him to his heart.

III

Love the Source of Righteousness

"All thy commandments are righteousness."—David

"Love is the fulfilling of the law."—Paul

Love is the one attribute of God, from which all other attributes spring—the all in all of God; and therefore the past, with its faults and failures, and the future, with its fears, if we but trust him, rest safely in Love's hands. But, says one, why is it so important to know this?

To say nothing of the unspeakable joy of this knowledge, all the power of the gospel of Christ to transform the soul and work in us the works of righteousness, depends upon it. All the righteousness of God is summed up in the ten commandments, wherefore David says: "The law of the Lord is perfect;" and, "all thy commandments are righteousness." God says, "Hearken unto me, ye that know righteousness, the people in whose heart is my law." Thus it is seen that to have the righteousness of God in the heart is simply to have the law of God written there. Jesus sums up all the law, and consequently the whole moral duty of man, in the two principles of love to God and love to man. John reduces these principles to the one principle of love to God, by showing that if we love God, the Father, we will love man, his child, our brother.[1] So Paul sums up the whole duty of man and all the righteousness of God in one word, saying "Love is the fulfilling of the law," and John assents to this proposition by saying, "Whoso keepeth his word, in him verily is the love of God perfected." Thus love dwelling in the heart of man is the fulfilling of all righteousness, and hatred dwelling there is the fulfilling of all iniquity, and all the conflict of the ages is simply the conflict of these two principles in the hearts of God's creatures.

But what is to change our hearts, that are so full of hatred, into hearts that are filled only with love? What is the source of all this love? John answers by saying, "Love is of God; and every one that loveth is born of God." Ah, that is it; like begets like—the mighty, constant, all-encompassing love of God, that upholds us, and enfolds us, and wraps us in with him, begets a like love in our hearts, leading us to reach out helpful hands in pitying, sympathetic love to all his creatures! And this is righteousness, the righteousness of God, and nothing else is righteousness.

Suppose it were possible for a man to do right simply that he might gain heaven. That very desire cherished persistently and thoughtlessly, when so many others are going down to death, would itself be selfishness and sin. Jesus Christ gave up heaven, accounting it not a thing to be held fast when man was lost.[2] Suppose it were possible that one should do right for fear of hell; that at best would be a species of cowardice, that dare not go where it believed so many others were going. All this would be but an external righteousness, a making clean the outside of the cup and the platter. The real principle of righteousness, which is love itself, would be lacking, and so there would be none of God's righteousness, but only self-righteousness, which is as filthy rags in his sight. There is truth and beauty in the old legend of an angel with a watering pot in one hand and a censor in the other, pouring water on the flames of hell, and causing the smoke to rise and obscure the glory of heaven, that men might do right simply for the love of right.

Let it be remembered that love of right and love of God are one and the same, for in the conception of all true men God is the embodiment of the supremely right, the supremely good. If, then, the love of God is the very soul and substance of all righteousness, how shall we love him?

Better ask, Why, when he is the one altogether lovely, do we love him so little? Why so much cold philosophy, and so little warm heart religion? Why have we come to think that the very word *love,* when applied to God, means a different thing from the warm reaching out of the heart's sympathies and longings which we feel toward a friend? Perchance, when applied to him, it means a mixture of awe and reverence more nearly approaching to fear and even terror than to love. Ah! all this comes from having false and pagan ideas of God; we have not yet seen that God is love. When we have, perfect love will cast out fear, because fear hath torment.

But says one, "How shall I love God? I have tried and tried." Poor soul! try no longer. Love does not come in that way. It is not pushed out from within by any sort of resolution; it is drawn out from without, by the sight of that which is lovely and lovable. Stop; cease thy struggling and trying; *look at Him* as revealed in his work and his word. Is he not the chiefest among ten thousand, the Rose of Sharon, the Lily of the Valley, the One altogether lovely? Do not thine eyes, even now, behold the King in his beauty? God knows full well that all righteousness is simply love to him, and he knows it is impossible for us to make ourselves love that which is not lovable; so creation and redemption are twin efforts of the divine One to reveal his mighty love to the soul that will but stop to look and live. It is his love that painted for thine eyes the blush of beauty on the rose's cheek. To regale[3] thy sense he gave that rose its perfumed breath. The delicate tints and traceries[4] of the thousand forms of beauty in thy path are so many evidences of his loving care—a care that, comprehending all, stoops from sweeping stars and suns to note the sparrow's fall. Ah, he it is that piles yon sunset clouds into such wondrous forms of temple and palace and pyramid, pouring over all such floods of golden light, to gild the very edge of darkness, that through these fairy gateways we almost fancy there lies the city of our hopes and dreams, and all our aspirations and longings seem not far to reach and realize! Does not his voice speak to thee in all this, telling thee that in the very closing in of the night of sorrow and darkness and death there may come to thee the bursting of a fairer day?

Is it not his love of which the birds sing? and from the murmuring of the wind-swept pine breaks not his sighing sympathy on thy soul? The ceaseless beating of the ocean on the rocky beach, what is it but the throbbing of his mighty heart against the barriers of selfishness and sin that hold thee from him? Listen! does not that heart beat in sympathy with human sorrow and human pain? do not those mighty arms reach out to enfold and encompass every land? "Why sayest thou, O Jacob, and speakest, O Israel, My way is hid from the Lord, and my judgment is passed over from my God? Hast thou not known? hast thou not heard? that the everlasting God, the Lord, the Creator of the ends of the earth, fainteth not, neither is weary? there is no searching of his understanding." We must not limit his care or set bounds to his love.

He who holdeth the worlds in the hollow of his hand, he who "bringeth out their host by number" and "calleth them all by names by the greatness of his might, for that he is strong in power; not one faileth," he it is that saith, "Comfort ye, comfort ye my people." He it is who puts our tears in his bottle, and writes them all in his book. O that men would look and listen till the thought of God revealed in nature's myriad forms, and speaking through her varied voices, might thrill their own hearts with his divine love! Then would the loneliness and the isolation of the hungry soul be gone, and above and below and round about us, enfolding us and wrapping us in with him, should we feel and know the sympathetic presence of that mind whose power upholds the universe, but whose love listens to the softest sigh of sorrow. Then with Carlisle might we well say, "Ah, sweeter than the mother's voice to the child that strays bewildered on the trackless world, comes this evangel to my heart! The universe is no longer dead and demoniacal, a charnel[5] house peopled with specters, but godlike, and my Father's."

And what can we say here of the revelation of God's love in redemption? With what words shall we speak, even afar off, of the unspeakable? This we can say with Paul, Who shall separate us from that love? "Shall tribulation, or distress, or persecution, or famine, or nakedness, or peril, or sword? Nay, in all these things we are *more than conquerors* through him that loved us. For I am persuaded, that neither death, nor life, nor angels, nor principalities, nor powers, nor things present, nor things to come, nor height, nor depth, nor any other creature, *shall be able to separate us* from the love of God, which is in Christ Jesus our Lord." But rather that, Christ dwelling in our hearts by faith, we may be rooted and grounded in love, and be able to comprehend with all saints what is the breadth, and length, and depth, and height, and to know the love of Christ, that passeth knowledge, *that we may be filled with all the fullness of God.*

Yes, to know the love of God is to be filled with his fullness, for God is love. All goodness, all righteousness is, love, and love is born of love, the human of the divine; so the all-important thing to know is that God is love. To know this is life eternal.

Notes:

1. 1 John 4:20.
2. Phil. 2:5–7.
3. To entertain sumptuously, to feast.
4. Ornamental work with branching lines; decorative interlacing of lines.
5. Charnal. A building or chamber in which bodies or bones are deposited—called also charnel house.

IV

Satan's Effort to Hide God's Love From Hungry Human Hearts

"When he speaketh a lie, he speaketh of his own: for he is a liar, and the father of it."

—John 8:44

All true righteousness is simply the dwelling of the divine love in the human heart and its consequent manifestation in human action. It is utterly impossible for anyone to love anything simply by resolving or trying to do so. Love is born of love; it is kindled in the soul by beholding and knowing Him who is lovable.

As therefore all redeeming power—all power to make righteous—is the power to beget love in the human soul, and as this can be done only by the manifestation of greater love, it follows that all of God's power to redeem the world is simply his power to manifest his mighty love for humanity. This agrees with what John says, "We love him because he first loved us," and "God so loved the world, that he gave his only begotten Son," etc. Because of these facts, we have seen that creation and redemption are both efforts of God to manifest his love to his creatures.

Now the converse of all this is that the power of Satan to defeat the work of God in the human soul is simply his power to defeat the manifestation of God's love; and just as the original proposition is proved by all of God's dealings with humanity, so also this is proved by every effort of Satan to thwart the divine plan. Every false doctrine and every false system of worship introduced into the world by Satan, we shall see, if we look at them carefully, have had for their one sole object the making the whole story of the love of God a lie.

In the very beginning Satan said to Eve, "Yea, hath God said, Ye shall not eat of every tree of the garden?" In the original this "yea" is simply an expression of contempt or scorn. When Eve answered, "We may eat of the fruit of the trees of the garden; but of the fruit of the tree which is in the midst of the garden, God hath said, Ye shall not eat of it, neither shall ye touch it, lest ye die," Satan said again in contempt of God, "Ye shall not surely die; for God doth know that in the day ye eat thereof, then your eyes shall be opened, and ye shall be as gods, knowing good and evil." This was a direct denial of God's love. God had placed that tree there in love, for the good of his children, to furnish an opportunity for the development of character, which would otherwise, in their then present state, be impossible. In love he had said, Ye must not eat of it, even as the father says to the child, You must not eat of these berries, my son, they are poison. Satan knew all this, but denied it, to make it appear that God, in envy or jealous fear, was refusing his children something which was for their good, and which would elevate them to an equality with him. Satan *lied,* and by that lie he brought from Christ himself the indignant denunciation of being a "liar from the beginning, and the father of it."

It is not too much to say that all false religion is a logical development from that lie, although we cannot here take time and space to show this definitely. No matter how many gods they worshiped, every civilized pagan nation has had a tradition, more or less vague and fanciful perhaps,—a tradition forgotten by the multitude, it may be, and only cherished by the *elite,* the educated few, and yet a tradition still,—that there is one God back of all these gods, who made them, and who made all things. Why did they not worship him?—Because they did not believe that he cared for them. They thought him so great and so far away that the human soul was beneath his notice, that the crushing out of all the race of man would be no more to him than the crushing of a worm to us.

And because this God was so far away, they went on inserting gods and demigods, and kings and priests between him and the human heart, till no sorrowing, suffering soul would ever think or dare to reach up the trembling hand of faith for the soothing, sympathetic touch of him who was truly and really divine. To such a world as this Jesus came to reveal the true God, and the God he revealed was Emanuel, *God with us;* and to such a people as this Paul taught the sublime truth that God is "not far from every one of us; for in him we live, and move, and have our being; . . . for we are also his offspring."[1]

The same thing that Satan accomplished in paganism he has also accomplished in the papacy. To papists, God is the stern, the distant judge, incapable of human sympathy or love, and Christ the mediator and intercessor, whose duty it is, if possible, to touch the heart of God with a feeling of our needs, and arouse his compassion. But even Christ is not touched with the feelings of all our infirmities; so he must be approached through the mediation of the Virgin, his mother, and of canonized saint, and living pope, and bishop, and priest. Thus again God is placed far away, and the beautiful, the living fact of his love is denied. He is no more "our Father," who takes delight in giving good gifts to his children.

Every pagan religion has its sacrifice, and this sacrifice is derived from the true Sacrifice by which the world is to be redeemed, through a degeneracy from the true type of that sacrifice which God gave to man at the gate of forfeited Eden. But Satan has brought it around so that the pagan sacrifice means just the opposite of the true. The meaning of the true sacrifice is this: *"God so loved the world, that he gave* his only begotten Son." Every sacrifice truly offered was a revelation, an expression of that great sacrifice by which God was to give the pledge to all his intelligent creatures of all worlds *that he so loved them that, if need be, he would give his life to redeem them.* But the pagan sacrifice speaks of a god of wrath and anger, whose wrath must in some way be appeased, perchance by the blood of a lamb, or it may be only by the blood of a fair maid, or innocent child, or some other human victim. When he smells the freshly flowing blood, they believe his vengeance will be satisfied, he will be propitiated.

What shall we say of the false idea of the atonement, held even by many in the popular Protestant churches of today, and expressed in a late confession of faith in these words, "Christ died to reconcile the Father unto us"? This is not the place to enter into a discussion of that theme; suffice it to say that it is the pagan idea of sacrifice applied to Christianity. God, they think, was angry; he must pour forth his wrath upon some one. If upon man, it would eternally damn him, as he deserved; but this would interfere with God's plan and purpose in creating the worlds, so this must not be. And yet God must not be cheated of his vengeance; for this reason he pours it forth upon Christ, that man may go free. So when Christ died, he was slain really by the wrath and anger of the Father.

This is paganism. The true idea of the atonement makes God and Christ equal in their love, and one in their purpose of saving humanity. "God was in Christ, reconciling the world unto himself." The life of Christ was not the price paid *to the Father* for our pardon; but that life *was the price which the Father paid* to so manifest his loving power as to bring us to that repentant attitude of mind where he could *pardon us freely.* The contrast between the true and the false ideas is tersely stated by the prophet in these words: "Surely he hath borne our griefs and carried our sorrows; *yet we did esteem him* stricken, smitten of God, and afflicted."[2] Thus Satan has transformed the truth of God's love into a lie, and even infused this lie into the very doctrine of the atonement of Christ.

These are but illustrations of the nature and tendency of all false systems. They are the devil's designs to thwart the power and purpose of the divine love. The doctrine of inherent immortality—"ye shall not surely die"—on which all these false systems rest for their hope of the future, comes to its legitimate fruitage in the terrible God-defaming belief in eternal conscious misery for all the multitudes of the lost.

Again: Satan transforms the glorious love-revealing truth of God's eternal purpose in creation into the stern doctrine of "absolute decrees," which doctrine accuses God of creating the multitudes for hell, and without giving them any chance to escape, turning them hopelessly into the place which Satan has invented for them, the few who are saved being also saved by God's absolute decree, and so, of course, in spite of themselves. These two doctrines, inherent immortality and absolute decrees, combine to make the theology of the world what it has been and is, and this combination finds its fullest development in the teaching of what may be called the "Ultra Calvinism of the Scottish Kirk." What that was, Buckle, in his "History of Civilization," states as follows:—

> "The clergy boasted that it was their special mission to thunder out the wrath and curses of the Lord. In their eyes the Deity was not a beneficent being, but a cruel and remorseless tyrant. They declared that all mankind, a very small portion only excepted, were doomed to eternal misery. And when they came to describe what that misery was, their dark imaginations reveled and gloated in the prospect.

> In the pictures which they drew they reproduced and heightened the barbarous imagery of a barbarous age. They delighted in telling their hearers that they would be roasted in great fires, and hung up by their tongues. They were to be lashed with scorpions, and see their companions writhing and howling around them. They were to be thrown into boiling oil and scalding lead. A river of fire and brimstone, broader than the earth, was prepared for them; in that they were to be immersed; their bones, their lungs, and their liver were to boil, but never to be consumed. At the same time, worms were to prey upon them, and while these were gnawing at their bodies, they were to be surrounded by devils, mocking and making pastime of their pains. Such were the first stages of their suffering, and they were only the first; for the tortures, besides being unceasing, were to become gradually worse.
>
> "So refined was their cruelty that one hell was succeeded by another; and, lest the sufferer should after a time grow callous, he was moved on that he might undergo fresh agonies in fresh places. All this was the work of the God of the Scotch clergy. It was not only his work, but it was his joy and pride; for, according to them, hell was created before man came into the world. The Almighty, they did not scruple to say, had spent his previous leisure in preparing and completing this place of torture, so that when the human race appeared, it might be ready for their reception. Ample, however, as the arrangements were, they were insufficient, and hell, not being big enough to contain the countless victims incessantly poured into it, had, in these latter days, been enlarged. But in that vast expanse there was now no void, for the whole of it reverberated with the shrieks and yells of undying agony."

All this and much more might be given, and, incredible as it may seem, every expression is taken from sermons and books actually preached or read at that time. No real Christian need be told that this is the work of Satan to blind men to the love of God, which is the only power that can draw them to him and make them righteous. In contrast with all this, put the beautiful words of Whittier;—

"But still my human hands are weak
To hold your iron creeds;
Against the words ye bid me speak
My heart within me pleads.

"I walk with bare hushed feet the ground
Ye tread with boldness shod;
I dare not fix with mete and bound
The love and power of God.

"Ye praise his justice; even such
His pitying love I deem;
Ye seek a king, I fain would touch
The robe that hath no seam.

"Not mine to look where cherubim
And seraph may not see;
But nothing can be good in him
Which evil is in me.

"The wrong that pains my soul below,
I dare not throne above;
I know not of his hate,—I know
His goodness and his love.

"I know not what the future hath
Of marvel or surprise,
Assured alone that life and death
His mercy underlies.

"I know not where his islands lift
Their fronded palms in air;
I only know I cannot drift
Beyond his love and care."

Notes:

1. Acts 17:27, 28.
2. Isa. 53:4.

V

The Fatherhood of God

"After this manner therefore pray ye,
Our Father which art in heaven."

—Jesus

God is love; all his attributes are the attributes of love. His justice, his wisdom, his power, his mercy, and even his wrath and anger, are only different faces of the many-sided but all-embracing and eternal love. It follows that the motive of God's action must be ever love's own. Love has no motive of policy or pride; in fact it has but one motive, and that is love itself. Whatever love does is for love's sake, to give pleasure to the object loved, and thus to receive pleasure in return. With these thoughts in view, we ask the question, Why did God create this world and place man upon it? Why did he create at all, and why, having begun, did he continue his work till the infinite abysses of unfathomed space are all "throbbing and palpitant" with suns and circling worlds?

The inspired apostle gives the answer: "Thou art worthy, O Lord, to receive glory and honor and power; for thou hast created all things, and *for thy pleasure they are and were created.*"[1]

Some one may say, "Yes, God is selfish as we are; he did it all for his own pleasure." But it must be remembered that the pleasure of love is never selfish. The pleasure of love is to love and be loved,—so to manifest itself as to bring return of love. If the imagination may dare such flights, conceive of God before the work of creation was begun. God is love; he was love then, for he is the same yesterday, today, and forever. He inhabiteth eternity. He was love, but he was alone, and love alone is lonely. The infinite heart, with all its tenderness, its sympathy, its power of affection, was alone, locked up by itself, with no other possible means of expression, only by creation. This was why God created, *for his pleasure,*—for love's pleasure, that love might so express itself as to bring return of love.

Man was made in the image of God. This image was largely lost through sin, and is to be restored through redemption, for we are to be "renewed in knowledge after the image of him that created" us.[2] Thus we see that this image does not consist in outward form merely, but also in the inward facts of feeling and thinking and knowing.

What is it in the human heart that creates all our homes, and builds up and binds together every true family? We call it the desire for offspring, but what is the desire for offspring but the desire of love to express itself in such a manner, as to bring return of love from loving hands, and loving eyes, and loving voices? This is perhaps the strongest inherent desire of the human heart. Inherited from whom?—From God, when he made us in his image.

It has often been said that the true home is a little world in itself. It is this desire in the human heart that creates these little worlds everywhere, and makes them centers of light, and love, and joy, till this old earth, it sometimes seems, is akin to heaven. It was this desire in the heart of divine Love that created this world, and all worlds, and peopled them with intelligent beings, capable of appreciating his love and returning him joyful loving service.

He made the world for his pleasure. His loving, lonely heart sought expression by its only means, creation, and the universe is but the materialization of that divine thought of love. This is what we mean by the Fatherhood of God. Christ dwelt upon this more than upon any other truth. It was he that taught us to say, "Our Father which art in heaven." Oh, there is something in those words, "our Father," that seems to bring God so near that we know and feel that he will hear faith's faintest cry of sorrow and need, and see the smallest signal of distress! "Our Father"—what do the words mean? What but that, as we are the fathers of our children, so he is the Father of us all, only he is more willing and more tender.[3]

The father's pleasure is in the happiness and success of his children.

With every advance step of the son or daughter into new prosperity and usefulness, new and higher joy comes to the father's heart. So the "pleasure" of God is identical with the highest possible happiness of all his creatures. So long as in one world there shall be one individual who has not yet arrived at the highest heights of the happiness of which he is capable, so long there is some joy of which God is capable, that he has not yet reached. Thus love binds man's interests and God's interests, and man's happiness and God's happiness, in one; and step by step throughout the ages of the future, as the race of intelligent beings marches on through greater knowledge to grander joys, God himself will lead them and participate with them in that higher happiness. "They shall hunger no more, neither thirst any more; neither shall the sun light on them, nor any heat. For the Lamb which is in the midst of the throne shall feed them, and shall lead them unto living fountains of waters; and God shall wipe away all tears from their eyes."

So much for the future; but here it is comforting to remember that the same love that rejoices in our joy suffers also in our sorrow. Jesus was the man of sorrows, and acquainted with grief, because he bore *our* griefs and carried *our* sorrows. Our sympathies are so narrow! If any grief comes within the little circle of our family and friends, we feel it, but what is the wide world to us? The little lake may sometimes be tossed with tempests within its narrow vale, but if the sun shines there, it smiles peacefully from between its fringing trees, no matter how the storms may rage elsewhere. Not so with the great ocean, whose mighty arms encompass every land. It holds the great world to its heart. It feels the ague[4] thrill of every earthquake shock, and its waves toss high to the breath of every storm. So the Saviour took the suffering world in his arms, and held it to his heart. He put himself *en rapport* with humanity. The great toiling, sorrowing, struggling mass of human life lay heavily on his sympathetic soul. He bore our griefs, he carried our sorrows. He is the same today. "We have not an High Priest that cannot be touched with the feelings of our infirmities."

But what was Jesus in the world for?—To reveal the Father. He said, "I and my Father are one." "He that hath seen me hath seen the Father." He revealed a God who is "our Father," whose great heart of love ever beats in sympathy with a sorrowing, sin-sick humanity, and who loves us ever, even in our sins, because he made us that he might have some one to love.

Weary soul, why not come to him and confess your sin, and accept the comfort and the consolation of his love? Why stay away because of fear? Why fancy longer that he loves you only when *you* may chance to feel yourself that you have done well and nobly? Why think that days of penance and weeping are necessary after you have sinned before he will receive you?

Even now his arms are open for you. Even now the Saviour knocks at the door of your heart. Does the mother love the boy only when he is good, and forget and hate him when he is wayward? Does not her love cling to him ever, tenderer still in the darkest hour of his sin? Is it not the cord to draw him back to virtue and to joy?

So does not the goodness of God lead thee even now to repentance? Dost not thou hear him say to thee, "The mother may forget the child, but I will not forget thee"? O that we might ever realize that we are his children, and that he made us for the joy of loving us and of having us love him; and that, while self-exiled, feeding on the swine's husks of earthly hopes and pleasures, he mourns us as his children still, though lost, ever holding himself ready to run and meet us a long way off on our return, and greet us with kisses of joy?

To realize this is to know God, and to know him is to love him, and this is life eternal.

Notes:

1. Rev. 4:11.
2. Col. 3:10.
3. Matt. 7:11.
4. A fit of shivering.

VI

The Glory of God

"How would it make the weight and wonder less,
If, lifted from immortal shoulders down,
The worlds were cast on seas of emptiness.
In realms without a crown?"

—Jean Ingelow

Before leaving the subject of God's love as revealed in creation, let us consider one more text. Rev. 4:11 says that God created all things for his pleasure. We have learned what that pleasure was, and what it reveals to us of divine love.

In Isa. 43:7 God says of man, "I have created him *for my glory*." The glory of God is not a mere external glory of rainbows and radiant brightness upon which no eye can look. When Moses, emboldened by God's precious promise of his presence and rest, sought to draw still nearer the Lord, and dared to make still greater requests, he said, "I beseech thee, show me thy glory." In reply, instead of blinding Moses' eyes by removing the black cloud that obscured his brightness, the Lord said, "I will make all my goodness pass before thee." Then the Lord descended in the cloud,. . . and proclaimed the name of the Lord. "And the Lord passed by before him, and proclaimed, The Lord, The Lord God, merciful and gracious, long-suffering, and abundant in goodness and truth." This, then, according to his own express declaration, is God's true glory—*his goodness.*

The external glory is but the result and outward manifestation of his goodness; and without this goodness the rainbow round about the throne would fade, and the unspeakable brightness, now mercifully shaded from mortal eyes, would pale into sickly glory flickering down into darkness.

When Moses knew this, he made haste, and bowed his head toward the earth, and worshiped; and so will we. O that the whole world might see it and know it! that they might turn with loving obedience to him! that, beholding the glory of his goodness, they might see therein revealed their selfishness and sin! Then with Job might they say, "I have heard of thee by the hearing of the ear; but now mine eye seeth thee. Wherefore I abhor myself, and repent in dust and ashes." It was thus to reveal God that Jesus came.

God made man "for his glory,"—for his goodness. That is, God, because of his glory—his goodness—because he is Love, made man a sentient, intelligent, morally responsible, and morally appreciative being, that he might reveal to him and in him his own goodness and glory; that man might thus, by returning to God due meed[1] of love and thanksgiving, be "to the praise of the glory of his grace." And all this will be accomplished in spite of sin and sorrow; for Paul says, "I reckon that the sufferings of this present time are not worthy to be compared with the *glory* which shall be revealed *in us*." And that this glory is the glory of the divine goodness to be revealed *in his children*, he shows by immediately adding, "The earnest expectation of the creature waiteth for the manifestation of the *sons of God*." If this glory—this goodness—can be revealed in us, all other glory will follow in due time.

But God created us to reveal this glory *to* us and *in* us. In the beginning he placed our infant race under angelic tuition,—children standing before the mighty mysteries of creation, every fact of which, as it should open before them, would reveal a Father's love, a Father's goodness, a Father's glory.

The child may awake to consciousness in a palace, surrounded by attendants and everything for his comfort, but with the father absent. At first his wants are purely physical. He needs but to eat and sleep; and the food is provided, and the means of rest. By and by the intellect begins to awaken, and it demands food for thought. The child wanders into another room, and finds shelves of books suited to his needs, and as his mind develops, demanding stronger food, he discovers volume after volume,—a magnificent library, every book stored with the grandest thoughts of the greatest thinkers. Among others he discovers a beautiful volume, every word of it written in letters of love,—an autobiography of his father's life, telling when he built the palace, where he is now, why he is absent, and when he will return.

By and by the love of the beautiful, the basis of all art, begins to manifest itself in the child, and to demand satisfaction. Behold, one day the boy tries a key in a neglected door of the great mansion, and lo, a splendid gallery of art, a little world in itself, created for him by gifted hands, and brought together here into this cosmos of beauty for his enjoyment. Beyond it is a music room with various instruments inviting him, and gifted musicians by their own sweet songs teaching him to touch the first notes. With the consciousness of every new need comes the discovery of the means of its satisfaction, till every day the child is compelled to say with surprise, "Father knows, father loves me, and has provided for every want."

Such a palace is this world, with its music and its varied beauty of mountain and valley, its gorgeous glories of sunset clouds, and its moonlit, star-gemmed evening skies! It is true an enemy has crept into this palace, and now some of the doors are locked, to be opened only by golden keys. But we know that the Father has provided means for the speedy extermination of this selfish fiend; and even now we can see Love's original purpose through it all,—that every want should be satisfied, and every noble desire gratified. There is beauty for the eye, and the eye for beauty; music for the ear, and the ear for music; fragrance for the nostril, and the nostril for fragrance; sweet for the taste, and the taste for sweet; and the dear Father made and mated them all.

Not all the growing needs of this mighty family can ever get one whit in advance of Love's omniscient forethought, that guided his hand at creation's dawn. When the wood is insufficient for fuel, and the candle for light, the coal and oil are discovered in another room in the palace, where Father stored them long ago. At every thoughtful step we have to say, "Father knows, and Father loves."

Why is all this?—Because God created this world and the universe for his pleasure and his glory, and Love's pleasure and glory is so to manifest itself as to receive return of love from loving, willing hearts. God created all the world by Jesus Christ.[2] "All things were made by him [Christ]; and without him was not anything made that was made." "He was in the world, and the world was made by him, and the world knew him not."[3] He made but one family in this world in the beginning, that "all nations of men for to dwell on all the face of the earth" might be of one blood.[4] Jesus Christ was the Father of that one family which was to people this world. He was also the Father of the families which were to people all other worlds, so that in him the inhabitants of all worlds find a common Father and a universal brotherhood of being. Thus it was designed that all intelligent beings should constitute but one family, and that Christ should be the Father. This is what the prophet means when he says of Jesus: "For unto us a child is born, unto us a son is given; and the government shall be upon his shoulder; and his name shall be called Wonderful, Counselor, The Mighty God, THE EVERLASTING FATHER, The Prince of Peace."[5]

But Jesus himself was the only begotten Son of the Father. So God the Father is our Father through Christ; and the inhabitants of all worlds were to be one brotherhood, one family, in him, that God through Christ might reveal *to* them and *in* them his love and his goodness, that they might behold his glory; for it pleased the Father that in him (Christ) should all fullness dwell.[6]

Of this family and this love Paul speaks when he says: "For this cause I bow my knees unto the Father of our Lord Jesus Christ, of whom the whole family in heaven and earth is named, that he would grant you, according to the riches of his glory, to be strengthened with might by his Spirit in the inner man; that Christ may dwell in your hearts by faith; that ye, being rooted and grounded in love, may be able to comprehend *with all saints* what is the breadth, and length, and depth, and height; and to know the love of Christ, which passeth knowledge, "that ye might be filled with all the fullness of God."[7]

This glory—this goodness—this love—which God sought to reveal to his children in creation, has been obscured by sin, and by sorrow, the result of sin, but a voice sweeter than the mother's voice to the suffering child says, "Comfort ye, comfort ye my people." "Every valley shall be exalted, and every mountain and hill shall be made low; and the crooked shall be made straight, and the rough places plain; and the glory of the Lord shall be revealed, and all flesh shall see it together." That voice is Jesus' voice, and by him the work will be accomplished, and the original purpose of creation, with all its love, stand revealed.

O, the deep, dark valleys of humiliation and suffering we are sometimes called to pass through,—lowest of all, the valley of the shadow of death! Yet his love shall light the way, and the valley by his presence shall be exalted into the very gates of heaven. The high mountains of human misery that have cast their baleful shadow on our lives, shutting out the sunshine of heaven from our hearts, will be brought low.

What has seemed to us so crooked and unjust here,—the prosperity of the wicked, the adversity of the righteous, those mysterious providences which sometimes seem like chance, and tempt us to think that He knoweth not our griefs, nor careth for our sorrows,—all this will be made clear and straight. And the rough ways over which our bruised and bleeding feet have trod so wearily, these, too, shall be made plain. Our eager eyes, scanning the rugged pathway, shall behold traces of his bloody footprints; and from the distant heights, whither he, too, has ascended through suffering, we shall hear his voice saying, "Come unto me, and I will give you rest." United with him, God shall wipe away all tears from our eyes.

All this will be accomplished, for this was God's pleasure in creation. Sin may seem to have thwarted his plan for a time; but "help has been laid upon One who is mighty," and "the pleasure of the Lord shall prosper in his hands."

Notes:

1. A fitting return or recompense.
2. Heb. 1:2.
3. John 1:3,10.
4. Acts 17:26.
5. Isa. 9:6.
6. Col. 1:12–19.
7. Eph. 3:14–19.

VII

The Unity of the Law and the Gospel

"The law of the Lord is perfect, converting the soul."

—David

God created all things by Jesus Christ, and therefore Christ is the "mighty God," the "everlasting Father" of all intelligent beings in all worlds. God the Father is the Father of Christ, and therefore through him of all these beings created by Christ. Thus God, Father and Son, unite in themselves all the morally accountable beings in the universe into one family; and it was the design that we should know and own our brotherhood, not only to all men, but to angels and the inhabitants of all worlds.

Now the All-Father gave to his children certain rules or laws to regulate their conduct. These laws were not arbitrary, not designed to show his right or power to boss, or domineer, over his children, but, like the rules of all well-regulated families, they were designed to promote the happiness of all the children, and the unity of the family life.

Although many might hesitate to express it thus, the thought that lingers in their minds is about like this: "God is arbitrary and obstinate, and will not permit the slightest variation from his laws without plunging us into eternal death." This is what Satan has ever said of God and of his government. I desire to show the contrary so that all may see. I desire to show that it is the variation itself that plunges us into eternal death, and not the arbitrary decree of God. It is the love of God that will not in any way countenance that variation, because it leads to such terrible results.

The law of God is not simply his fiat; it rests on eternal principles of pleasure and pain,—principles as unchangeable in their very nature as the laws that govern the seasons or control the motions of the planets. The law is not so simply because God said so, but he said so because it was so, and because it must eternally and universally be so.

On the correct understanding of these principles of the nature of God's law depends our power to comprehend God's love in all his dealings with his creatures. On this rests the whole philosophy of the purpose of creation and of the plan of redemption. The existence of misery and suffering, the need for an atonement, and how that atonement is accomplished by Christ, can be understood in the light of God's love only as the nature of his law stands revealed. It is for this reason that we purpose to dwell at some length in these pages on the nature of God's law.

We have always thought of the ten commandments as requiring our love to God and to all his creatures; have we ever thought of them as an expression of his love to us? It would be absolutely foolish to demand our love by arbitrary fiat; love cannot be given in that way; love is born only of love. The state might as well legislate that the sun should not shine or that water should not flow downhill, as for the Lord to make such arbitrary demand for love. In either case the law could not affect in the slightest the thing legislated about.

Yet it remains true that all the law of God requires is love, and that, as the apostle says, love is the fulfilling of the law,—of the whole law. How is this?—Simply that the law itself, when we understand it, is a revelation of such infinite love as to beget within us a returning, responsive love that can and will fulfill the law.

"God is love." Every word, every jot and tittle, of that law, coming from love, requires only such service as love dictates. When the same love which that law expresses to us is begotten by it in our hearts, and flows out toward God and all his creatures in loving actions, then the law is fulfilled.

It may be objected that the divine love, to beget returning love in us, is revealed, not in the law, but only in the life and death of Jesus Christ. In one sense this is true, and in another it is not true. The love that God sought to reveal in his law, and throughout all the administration of that law in his government, has been denied by Satan from the beginning; "for he is a liar," "and abode not in the truth." It has also been so obscured and hidden by sin and sorrow that many have not beheld it. But the love of God as revealed in Jesus Christ *is no new love for us*. God is the same; "with him is no variableness, neither shadow of turning." All this love for us he had from the beginning, and he expressed it in his law; only the devil denied it, and sin obscured it. Christ simply revealed the love that God had ever borne us, and that underlies all his laws and government.

The life of Christ is the law of God in action; his death, but the natural result of perfectly keeping that law, and perfectly proclaiming it to others, in a world that hated truth and goodness. Look at that life and death of immaculate love. In all this did Christ do more than the law requires?—Impossible, for then he were more than perfect; for the psalmist says, "The law of the Lord *is perfect*." Christ's life, then, reveals no new love, but to hearts that were hardened and to eyes that were blinded by sin he reveals anew the same love which dictated every word of that law.

There is no conflict between Sinai and Calvary. "Thy law is the truth," said David, and "all thy commandments are righteousness." Again, "Make me to go in the path of thy commandments." Jesus was the "righteous servant" who was to justify many by his righteousness. He says, "I am the *way*, the *truth,* and the *life*." He was and is the Prince of Peace and the manifestation of mercy. In him "mercy and truth are met together; righteousness and peace have kissed each other."

We have seen that all created intelligent beings find a common Father, and hence a universal brotherhood, in God; now we wish to see that all of God's dealings with his morally accountable creatures are simply the dealings of a loving parent with his children. This must be so if he is "our Father." Is he not a good Father? The very word *God* means good. If he be convicted of being other than good in anything, he is no longer God. This were to dethrone him, and then—

"Who the orphaned moons doth lead,
And who the unfathered spheres?"

Is he not love? and can love act other than lovingly? To show that God acts from other motive than love is to show that he is not God, for "God is love." Hear him: "Ye are my witnesses, saith the Lord, *that I am God*." Have we always witnessed thus? Have we not all in our hearts a thousand times doubted his love, while believing fully in the love of some human friend? Ah, this is to exalt the human above the divine—this is idolatry!

Perchance our lives have been sad and dark, and we have wondered why, and thus been led to doubt. Jesus was the only begotten Son of the Father, loved by him before the worlds were, and yet while here he was a "Man of sorrows and acquainted with grief." He, the Captain of our salvation, was "made perfect through suffering." This is the ministry of sorrow. Do you not know, sorrowing and tempted one, that the shadow cannot fall except the sun be shining overhead? "When the mists have cleared away," and we see the Father's face, and know as we are known, ah, then we shall see that—

"Darkness in the pathway of man's life
Is but the shadow of God's providence,
By the great Sun of wisdom cast thereon;
And what is dark below will be light in heaven."

VIII

The Nature of the Divine Government

" 'My times are in thy hand;'
Why should I doubt or fear?
My Father's hand will never cause
His child a needless tear."

—William F. Lloyd

God is "our Father," and it was his design that we should recognize him as such, and that, thus united in him, all intelligent beings should find a universal brotherhood. This being true, it follows that God's laws and his methods of enforcing them—in short, all of his dealings with us in this world—are those of a loving, wise parent with his children.

Take a common, homely illustration. The little boy wants to eat the unripe fruit. Why?—Because of the pleasure of eating it. The fact is, looking at it in the broadest sense, pleasure—happiness—is the universal quest of life. With this problem all religions and philosophies have to deal.

Epicurianism teaches its votaries to seek pleasure in the fleeting phantoms of the passing hour. Stoicism seeks to make men indifferent to the desire for happiness—that is, strange as it may seem, it seeks to make men contented or *happy* without happiness. Buddhism teaches that conscious existence is misery, and that therefore happiness is unattainable save in *nirvana*, or extinction of being, by absorption into Deity.

It is to the honor of Christianity that it taught the only possible way to gain this universal quest. We are to find it by forgetting it; and we are to forget it for ourselves in the eager desire to gain it for those around us. Happiness is a coy maiden that ever eludes the too-eager grasp of the selfish seeker; but when self is forgotten in the service of others, the thrilling heart becomes conscious of her presence, and the eye, for a moment uplifted, rests full on her smiling face.

But to return to the illustration. The boy in his desire to eat the green apple only takes into consideration the few minutes it takes to eat it. He is forgetful of the future in the desire for the present pleasure. The father says, "Stop, child; don't eat that apple." Why this prohibition? Is it that the father wishes to exercise his authority?—No. The father loves the child. He takes more time into consideration than the boy. He thinks not only of those few minutes while the taste of the apple is in the mouth, but he thinks of the morrow of sickness and pain, and possible death, and in love he says, "Thou shalt not."

Suppose the child is caught again eating the fruit. The father says to him, "Johnnie, if you eat another one of these apples, I shall whip you." Why is this? Is the father angry with the child? and does he propose to retaliate by whipping?—Ah, no! He says in his heart: "The boy does not fully understand my reason for refusing him that coveted pleasure; but *he must not eat that fruit*, it will kill him. I will give him a motive for refraining that he will understand."

All this is love on the part of the parent. To the child at the time it may seem arbitrary and hard, but when he comes to look at it from the standpoint of the father and to know why he forbade, he will thank and love him for the prohibition.

This is also the way God is dealing with us. We are children down here in the darkness. We see only such a little way, enshrouded as we are with these shadows. Our life, looked at with other than the eye of faith, "is a narrow vale between the cold and barren peaks of two extremities." "We strive in vain to look beyond the heights." At the best, in the beginning we only take into consideration this little life, bounded by the narrow span between the waking and the sleeping.

But this is only the *today* of our existence. The tomorrow—ah, that tomorrow! how in God's sight it opens out for us into the great deep sea of eternity! Eternity! who can tell us what it holds for us? for it, too, comes from a Father's loving hand, and brims with his blessings. What possibilities of pleasure are here, o'ertopping our highest dream! "Eye hath not seen, nor ear heard, neither have entered into the heart of man, the things which God hath prepared for them that love him."

But all these possibilities of the tomorrow depend upon the right use of the today. God sees the end from the beginning. He knows what he has for us in those dim distances beyond the utmost reach of our vision. He sees the ages rising before us, and us rising to meet them, with ever-increased capacity for happiness, and yet that capacity ever full to overflowing. God knows the only path that leads that way, and that is the path of righteousness. He says in love, "This way, my child, this way."

Broad and many are the ways that lead to death. How often, caught by the glare of some present promise of pleasure, we turn aside into some of these paths, only to hear the Father say, "Thou shalt not, my child, thou shalt not!" If on what seems to be the sunny slope of sensual and selfish indulgence we ever see the sign set up, "No Trespassing Here," the Father's hand set it there to turn us back into the path that leads to the source of the sunshine.

Satan would ever tempt us to forget the future, with its boundless possibilities, in the pursuit of the fickle present, with its fleeting joys. He never raises the crystal goblet of bliss to the human lip but to dash it at the feet as soon as a single drop is quaffed,[1] and then he stands pointing at the broken fragments with a fiendish laugh. All the baits with which he tempts the soul to sin are but the fabled bag of gold at the end of the bow of promise. As we pursue, the bow recedes before us, and finally it vanishes out of sight in the blackness of the coming storm, and even the promise of pleasure is gone.

Thus men forsake the Lord, the only true fountain of living water, to follow some tempting mirage into the desert. On and on they go, unmindful of the lengthening shadows, stimulated ever by a thirst which only the living water can satisfy, and by which God intended to lead them to him. By and by the mirage itself vanishes with the setting sun, and the soul finds itself alone in the gathering darkness, surrounded only by the barren sands of a misspent life.

Hear the testimony of one who had traveled this way to the very verge of the precipice of despair, catching at each new promise, and trusting last of all only to the solace of human affection. As this last object of his hope and trust was slipping from his grasp, irresistibly drawn by the cruel clutch of consumption, he breaks forth into this plaint:[2]—

"What is our love with its tincture of lust,
Its pleasures that pain us, its pain that endears,
But joy in an armful of beautiful dust,
That crumbles and flies on the wings of the years."

God would not have us trust to these fleeting pleasures. All that there is of true happiness, even here, comes from him.[3] His law reveals those principles, obedience to which makes happiness possible both here and hereafter. He is ever seeking to persuade us to live and act, not in the todays and tomorrows as they come and go, but in eternity with him.

His law is the highway of holiness over which the ransomed shall walk when they return and come to Zion with songs and everlasting joy, to obtain joy and gladness, while sorrow and sighing flee away. It is to turn us into this way that he in love afflicts us here. Once in this way, the path rises and broadens before us, reaching upward through limitless vistas, till lost in the glory that surrounds the throne.

Herbert Spencer, in his "Data of Ethics," says that the basis of ethical distinctions is not the revealed will of God. Man does not need any such revelation. He can through experience evolve his own law. Then he goes on to show that every right principle is right because it tends to the happiness of all created intelligent beings, and that every wrong principle is wrong because it tends to their misery. In this he thinks he has done away with the need for a revelation of the divine will; and as he fancies there is no need, so he denies the fact of such a revelation.

Who does not see that his logic, instead of denying the need for such a revelation, simply lifts that revelation above the realm of mere arbitrary decree, into the region of fatherly love? True, the boy, if he did not die of the *cholera morbus*, might through much pain have discovered that eating unripe fruit did not tend to happiness. The father's love would save him that misery. If there was no tempting devil, man through countless ages of suffering, and when generation after generation had been hopelessly lost without ever having discovered the right way,—man might at last rise to something of a knowledge of these principles on which happiness depends, and so "evolve his own law." But even then he would find himself so bound by the chains of evil habits already contracted, that the *good he would do, he could not*; and so even then he would need the Saviour, and the divine revelation of him.

God, in the revelation of his law, would save man all this, and give to the first man an equal chance of happiness and eternal life with that *last man*, which a science falsely so called ever babbles of as the hope of coming ages, the crown of evolution.

Yes, God's way is ever the best, for his way is love's own. The Father's love is not satisfied with making happiness possible merely to the *race*, after ages of misery and suffering, but to the individual as well, and brings the possibility of endless happiness to every hungering heart. This is the "why" for God's law. This is why he gave it to Adam in the beginning. This "why," like the reason for everything God does, is simply love, for God is love.

Notes:

1. To drink deeply.
2. Lamentation, wail.
3. James 1:16,.17.

IX

The Law of Love

"O marvelous credulity of man!
If God indeed kept secret, could'st thou know
Or follow up the mighty Artisan
Unless he willed it so?"

—Jean Ingelow.

It has been said that we should be satisfied to know *what* God says, *what* he does, and *what* he commands, without asking *why*. This last, it is thought, would be but to pry impiously into the secrets of God, and seek to fathom his motives. The reply is that the whole life of Christ and the whole inspired word is a revelation of the motive of God; and John condenses all this revelation into one word when he says, "God is *love*."

We may know a man's acts to a certain degree, and yet really know nothing of the man. Only as we know the motives which underlie these acts do we know him.

This is as true of God as of man. But God has invited us to know him; he has sought to reveal himself to us through Jesus Christ; and he has told us that in him are all the treasures of wisdom and knowledge. Jesus himself said, "This is life eternal, that they might know thee, the only true God, and Jesus Christ, whom thou hast sent." So this little book is a humble effort to look underneath the "what," and discover something of the "why" of God's deeds and words.

It is true this is holy ground, where one needs to walk, as did one of old, with bared feet and uncovered head. It is true, too, that it is a mystery into which the angels desire to look; but it is not a mystery because God is hiding it from us, but rather because it is the mystery of a love that passeth knowledge. Here are depths and heights and lengths and breadths that eternity will not be long enough for us to fully fathom, yet even now we may know them by faith. Certain it is that if God wishes to keep secret on any point, we shall have no fear of finding him out; but he is the Fountain of Life, and he has said that whosoever will may come and take *freely*.

The child knows full well that when he can see the love in the father's command, it is much easier to obey; so when the same divine love that dictated God's commands gets into our hearts, we shall know, with John, that "this is the love of God, that we keep his commandments; and his commandments are not grievous."

"Thou shalt have no other gods before me." Why this prohibition? It is true that God is our Creator, and that to him is due our supreme love and worship. It is true that he has a right to command it, and that we ought to yield it because he commands it. That right to command our love and worship rests, however, on his love to us, of which love this very command is a manifestation. Is there no higher reason here than that God, having a desire to be loved and worshiped, and having a right to our love and worship, commands it?

We might pause and ask why he desires our love. It is only love that longs for love. The heart that yearns with inexpressible tenderness over another, finds its own love the true measure of its longing for return of love. God's language to Israel, as they broke this precept, was ever that of wounded love. "My covenant they brake, although I was an husband unto them, saith the Lord." "Turn, O backsliding children, saith the Lord; for I am married unto you." "Surely as a wife treacherously departeth from her husband, so have ye dealt treacherously with me, O house of Israel, saith the Lord." All these expressions reveal the yearning love of God that underlies this precept. It is the longing of true love for the supreme affections of the object loved.

But there is a deeper and broader meaning here than this. Just as the happiness of the family depends upon their devotion to one another, so with the universal family of which we have spoken. When gazing upon the full moon sailing the upper sky and shedding its mellow light upon all around, have you never thought that some friend, though thousands of miles away, might at that instant also be looking on the same object? and was not the thought a mysterious cord to draw your hearts nearer together, in spite of the distance and the darkness? So the supreme look of love cast by each upon the one God was to draw the hearts of humanity nearer together, and hold them in happy unity.

When canvassing once in Western Iowa, the writer entered a house and began to exhibit his book. He had not proceeded far when the following conversation took place. The gentleman of the house, noticing something peculiar in his accent, said:—

"You are a Yankee, aren't you?"

"Yes; did you discover it from my speech?"

"Yes; what State are you from?"

"New Hampshire."

"*Is that so?* What county?"

"Hillsborough county."

"*I want to know!* Did you ever become acquainted with a man by the name of Hanson, who lives on the old Horace Greeley farm up in Amherst?"

"Yes; he is a friend of mine. I took dinner with him there at the old log house not long before I came West."

He rose from his seat, and extending his hand, which I grasped, while his lips quivered, and the tears ran down his face, he said:—

"That man is my brother. I have not seen him for thirty years. Wife, is not dinner most ready? I will take that book, Mr. Fifield, and you must stay with us to dinner."

I was a perfect stranger to that man, yet he treated me as a brother. He wanted me to stay with him a week, and come and see him when I could. What made us acquainted at once and united our hearts? We had a common object of affection, and each knowing and loving the same person, we knew and loved each other. So by uniting all men in the loving worship of one Father, God would make them all one happy family of brothers and sisters.

Illustrating this, there is a little story of a poor street waif who was admitted one cold morning into the back door of a house by a minister, who gave him a very small and very dry crust of bread, and then began to question him. The boy was very ignorant, and so the minister began to tell him about God. He said that God was the Creator, that he made all things, and that he lived in heaven. The boy, in his hunger, tried to eat the crust, hardly noticing what was said. Finally the minister made the casual remark that God was our Father. This caught the boy's attention. Said he, "Is he your Father?" The minister said, "Yes." "Is he my Father?" Again the minister said, "Yes." The boy thought a moment, then said, "You and me are brothers, are'nt we?" Reluctantly the minister said, "Yes." Then said the boy, "Aren't you ashamed to give me such a dry crust of bread?"

This story, simple as it is, may bring conviction and condemnation to many of us. Have we cherished the grace of brotherly kindness for all? Have we, in owning God as our Father, felt our relation and our duty to all his children? This little story carries the principle of the first precept in it; and in brief, of all the ten, for they are all included in the fatherhood of God and the brotherhood of man. The breaking of this precept has led to the worship of different gods. This has divided the world up into different families and different nations, each having its own gods, and each saying that the gods of the other nations were no gods, each owning its brotherhood to its own little tribe, or clan, but denying it to all others. Thus the world has been filled with war and bloodshed. Men have fought because they were jealous for the preeminence and supremacy of their gods; and so the very gods whom their fears and superstitions created, have taken part in the destruction of human life.

It is not too much to say that more misery has been caused by the direct violation of this commandment than by everything else. Indeed, when we come to remember that the other nine commandments are only special directions for the observance of the two principles contained in this precept, we shall then see that all sin, and therefore all misery, is the result of the violation of this commandment.

God knew in the beginning the inevitable result to his children of such departure from him. There was no selfishness in the love that said, "Thou shalt have no other gods before me." It was Jesus Christ who took up this precept and taught us to say, "Our Father which art in heaven." He would realize in the church what would have been realized in the world if it had not been for sin. To that church he said, "Call no man your father upon the earth; for one is your Father, which is in heaven." "Be not ye called Rabbi; for one is your Master, even Christ; and all ye are brethren."

With our divine Lord, God was always "our Father,"—a Father who delighted to give good gifts to his children,—a Father who fed the raven, and clothed the lily with beauty, and without whom not a sparrow fell to the ground. Jesus' whole life was an illustration of this precept. To him all men were brothers, and he sought to bring them to a recognition of that brotherhood. Though he came from the unspeakable glory that he had with the Father before the worlds were, yet he stooped to our needs, and was not ashamed to call us brethren.

O that we all might be like him; then would we be able to lead hungry-hearted, world-weary men and women to Jesus, that manifestation of divine love, where, born again of the one Father, they might indeed become members of the one true brotherhood! O that we might realize this brotherhood more fully now in our churches, so that the sympathetic response of heart to heart might ever spare a tear for one another's sorrow, and a smile for one another's joy! Then would our hearts not be, of necessity, locked up with sorrow's slow fire, smoldering in the darkness; but, even here, as He designed, there might be an image of heaven upon earth,—a place where we could meet, not merely face to face, but also heart to heart, and know as we are known. The love that would give us this joy is revealed in the first principle of the decalogue and illustrated in the life of Jesus Christ.

The "why" of that command is love, for "*God is love*."

X

The Two Ways

"Enter ye in at the strait gate; for wide is the gate, and broad is the way that leadeth to destruction, and many there be which go in thereat: because strait is the gate, and narrow is the way, which leadeth unto life, and few there be that find it."

—Matt. 7:13, 14

Having seen that the observance of the first precept of the decalogue is absolutely indispensable to the happiness of intelligent beings, we shall also see the same of all the others. In fact, the remaining three commands of the first table are only guards against the departure from the loving worship of the one Father; and the six precepts of the last table are indispensable directions for preserving the harmonious unity of the one brotherhood.

But who is this one Father?—He is the Creator of heaven and earth, and of all things. Any departure, therefore, from his worship to that of another god can be nothing else than the leaving of the Creator for the created, a forgetting of the worker in a false admiration for the work.

Every work begins in the mind of the worker. However great and wonderful it may be, it is only a revelation of that mind which, being capable of conceiving and executing such a work, is more wonderful still. All true appreciation of the works of God finds these works, in their infinite variety and beauty, but a golden and glorified stairway, over which, mounting breathlessly, the mind pauses not till, at the top, surcharged with inexpressible wondering approbation, it breaks forth into the ceaseless, "Holy, holy, holy, Lord God Almighty!" "Thou art worthy, O Lord, to receive glory and honor and power; for thou hast created all things, and for thy pleasure they are and were created!" All idolatry is a pausing somewhere in this ascent, to give the supreme adoration and love to some passing object, instead of mounting upward to him.

Then, there are not only the works of God, but the works of Satan, which are simply a defacement of the works of God, Satan himself being the chief deformity. From the point in the ascent godward where the mind pauses, refusing to ascend higher, Satan leads it from the admiration of the pure works of God to that of his own deformed works, and then gradually downward to him.

The second and fourth precepts of the decalogue were designed to be safe barriers against this sin. The Sabbath was a weekly memorial that the only true God, the only one worthy of worship, was the Creator of all things. "Remember the Sabbath day to keep it holy." Why?—"For in six days the Lord made heaven and earth, the sea, and all that in them is, and rested the seventh day; wherefore the Lord blessed the Sabbath day, and hallowed it."

Wherever in the Bible the object of the writer is to distinguish between false gods and the true God, this fact is alluded to. Paul says, "Every house is builded by some man; but he that built all things is God." Jeremiah says, "The gods that have not made the heavens and the earth, even they shall perish from the earth, and from under these heavens. He hath made the earth by his power, he hath established the world by his wisdom, and hath stretched out the heavens by his discretion."

To the Athenian idolaters, who, fearing they might overlook the worship of some deity and so incur his wrath, had erected an altar with this inscription, "To the Unknown God," Paul said, "Whom therefore ye ignorantly worship, him declare I unto you. God that made the world and all things therein."

It is a wonderful fact that the heathen nations have almost always admitted that their gods were part of the creation, and that they have had a shadowy idea of another God back of them, and above them, who was the Creator. If men had always kept the Sabbath in the true spirit of it, this false worship would have been impossible. Every week all men would have commemorated the fact that the only true God and Father of all was the Creator. Thus they would have continued in the worship of the one God, the one Father. It was to be a day for all minds to mount together that golden stairway, and find joyous communion together in him. Says the psalmist, in that song for the Sabbath day: "Thou, Lord, hast made me glad through thy work, I will triumph in the works of thy hands. O Lord, how great are thy works! and thy thoughts are very deep." This is the true spirit of the Sabbath day,—a day to forget the world and its cares, while soul with soul we soar to breathe the pure air of the heavenly heights.

There have ever been but two pathways,—the straight and narrow, leading upward; and the broad way, leading downward. When men worship the Creator, his work lies all around them, to show that he is higher than their highest dream of him.

There is an infinity in every sun and star and world, in every leaf and plant and flower, which man cannot comprehend. If the mind cannot fathom the work, how can it fathom the worker? How can it do other than say in humble devotion, "Great and marvelous are thy works, Lord God Almighty?" It must remember that its highest ideal of him is still only an ideal, and that God is far higher and grander. As by beholding we become changed into his likeness, till we attain near to that ideal, we can now build that ideal higher and truer. And so the soul plumes itself for another flight, ever upward, upward, from faith to faith, from glory to glory, till, lost in the limitless glorified distance, we are perfectly transformed into his image.

As thus we become sanctified through his truth, we not only become one with him, but one with each other. "Sanctify them through thy truth; . . . that they all may be one; as thou, Father, art in me, and I in thee, that they also may be one in us." These are the words of Jesus, and this is the spirit and object of all true worship. The nearer we come to him, the nearer we come to each other; the more we own him as our Father, the more we own each other as brethren and sisters, till, when the work is completed, Jesus says, "At that day ye shall know that I am in my Father, and ye in me, and I in you."

Ah, what blissful unity? This is the pathway that leads upward, in ever-increasing happiness, to God. This is why the Father said of this way, "Thou shalt." The "why" was love, for God is love.

But there is another pathway in which men have always been prone to walk. They have worshiped and served the creature more than the Creator. They have not only paused, in the ascent, to worship the created, but they have symbolized the created by the works of their own hands, and then worshiped their own ideal as thus represented. Thus they first refused to glorify God *as God*, by believing him to be still higher and better than their present conception of him, and so walking onward and upward in the opening light of his truth. On the contrary, by professing themselves to be too wise thus to walk, they did what men always do when they write out their creed,—they said in their hearts, "He is no higher than our present knowledge of him;" and so they became fools by changing the glory of the incorruptible God into an image made first like to corruptible man, then to birds, and fourfooted beasts, and creeping things, down, down, to that old serpent himself, which is the devil and Satan.

Thus Satan was put in the place of God; and men, by worshiping, instead of being led upward to unity in him, were led downward into all deformity and strife, hateful and hating one another, till every man's hand was against his neighbor, and the imagination of the thoughts of men's hearts was evil and only evil continually. This was the downward road that led to misery and death. God foreknew the result of every course of action. This is why he said in the second commandment of this course, "Thou shalt not." The "why" was love, for God is love.

For the same reason the third precept of the decalogue enjoins a reverential use of the name of God, that this sacred name may ever have a mysterious power to beget within us higher and truer conceptions of the object named, thus lifting us up to unity with him and with each other. Between these two paths, the one leading ever upward to limitless heights of life and joy and glory, the other downward through darkness to death, God placed the institution of the Sabbath. Its object was to obstruct the way of the downward path, and to turn men's feet into the upward way.

By this can be seen the malignant design of Satan in plucking that institution from its place and putting a false one in its stead. Just as the true Sabbath is a memorial of the power of the Creator to lift us ever upward to him, so the false sabbath is a symbol of the power of the created (of him who thought in it to exalt himself above all that is called God or that is worshiped) to drag us ever downward to death.

Which way shall we go, the way of love and light and glory, or the way of darkness, discord, and death?

XI

The Design of the Law

"Wide as the world is thy command,
Vast as eternity thy love;
Firm as a rock thy truth shall stand,
When rolling years shall cease to move."

—Isaac Watts

The first table of the law was designed, by keeping men in the worship of the one God and Father, to unite them in one family and lift them ever higher and higher, into the realization of all possible joy and peace.

The second table of the law was written by the same finger, and came from the heart of the same loving Father. It is simply his statement of the few brief principles which underlie all possible family unity and happiness in the relation of man with man. This is too apparent to need any argument. Even the civil law enforces, to some extent, the outward observance of the letter of these precepts as the basis of civil society. Upon such outward observance civil society rests, and without it the whole social fabric would crumble.

The difference between civilization and absolute savagery of the worst type is merely a difference made possible by such outward observance. When the majority of the people, of their own free will, at least outwardly, observe these commandments, and, combining together, form an influence strong enough to hold the fractious minority in check, then, and not till then, civilization is possible. But if the vast difference between civilization and savagery is due to the outward observance of the letter of that law, even that observance being forced upon the minority, what can be said of the possible joy in that ideal state where all, of their own free will, keep not the letter only but also the spirit of the law? What blissful friendships, what perfect security and confidence in all! Indeed, the inhabitants of that country might "dwell safely in the wilderness, and sleep in the woods." In just so much as we rise above the mere outward observance into the spiritual, are we lifted above the purely civil into the Christian.

It was through Jesus Christ that the Holy Spirit was given to us, to write the law, not merely in the letter, and on tables of stone, but in the spirit, and on the fleshly tables of the heart. In all this God had not only his own pleasure but the happiness of his children in view. The two were identical, for God is love. I repeat: The highest possible pleasure of God is identical with the highest possible happiness of all his creatures. The happiest family, other things being equal, is the one which honors father and mother most. The writer remembers a few such families, in which he has been privileged for a time to dwell,—remembers them as oases in the desert of life, as bright spots where heaven has indeed come down and touched this earth. If obedience to this precept will make one family happy, will it not two? will it not three? will it not all? This is why God enjoined it.

The commandment, "Thou shalt not kill," which, in the spirit, means, thou shalt not hate, guards the joy of living.

"Thou shalt not commit adultery," guards the sacred joys of the family relation.

"Thou shalt not steal," guards the right and joy of property.

"Thou shalt not bear false witness." This guards the right of property, and the joys of friendship and reputation.

"Thou shalt not covet," forbids the cherishing of the first germ of the desire that leads to all evil and all misery.

Why, how careful our Father is of us! how desirous for our utmost possible joy! This is love's solicitude.

Because of the breaking of these precepts the world is divided into the poor, with the endless o'erwearying struggle for existence; and the rich, with the haunting care of uncounted gold,—anxiety and unrest in both extremes, instead of plenty and pleasure for all. Because of the violation of these principles this world holds for us not one joy that is sure, not one hope that may not deceive, not one pleasure unmated with its possible pain. The transgression of these commands has made necessary our prisons, our insane asylums, and our poorhouses; it has put locks not only on our houses and shops, but on our hearts as well.

How often we are compelled to walk our way alone and lonely, though amid the crowd and throng of men! No human eye sees our sorrow or sympathizes with our joy; the heart's sacred temple is kept open only for phantom footfalls, ourselves the only worshipers at the shrine of its memories. If, perchance, to some trusted friend the outer door is left for a moment ajar, it is hastily closed and barred, lest some vandal hand snatch away, for the vulgar gaze, the picture from the wall or the statue from its niche.

Ah, how different this life we are compelled to lead here, because of sin, from that which were possible had these principles always been the rule of human action! True, the Holy Spirit, if we invite him, will make this heart's temple his abode, and even now fill and flood it with the light of that other world, where all our ideals and aspirations will be realized, and more than realized, in him. Still the heart will long for human sympathy. Did not Jesus in the hour of his drawing nearest to God, reach out with human longing for his disciples, and say, "Father, I will that they also whom thou hast given me, be with me where I am"?

The world is living in open disregard of the spirit, if not of the letter, of these precepts,—living in envy and jealousy, in strife and the struggle for vainglory, hateful and hating one another. But Jesus Christ says of his church, "They are not of the world, even as I am not of the world." They have been chosen out of the world, to have this law written in their hearts, and to walk the highway of holiness with him. That way is the way of peace, for Jesus is the Prince of Peace. Every step of the way will bring them not only nearer to God, but nearer to one another.

Even here the ransomed of the Lord may be seen returning, and coming to Zion with songs and everlasting joy upon their heads. But if sorrows do come, we, too, will bear one another's sorrows, and "heart to heart, we'll bide the shadows till the mists have rolled away." This is the principle that underlies the law,—the Father's loving desire for the welfare and happiness of his children. Every jot and tittle was dictated by love, for "God is love."

Here we have struck a foundation which Antinomianism[1] can never touch; now we know why the law can never change; it is because his love never changes. He is the same yesterday, today, and forever; and he has loved us with an everlasting love. Jesus says, "It is easier for heaven and earth to pass, than one tittle of the law to fail." This is no hyperbole; it is the simple statement of a fact that we can understand. There was a time when heaven and earth did not exist. It is conceivable that the time might come again when they would not exist. The God who made them could destroy them. This is thinkable, but it is absolutely unthinkable that any world ever did or could exist, peopled with intelligent beings, where the obedience of these principles would not lead to joy, and the disobedience of them to misery and death.

It is not thinkable that God could have one idea of right in Jupiter, and another in Saturn, and another somewhere else. He is the same God, not only yesterday, today, and forever, but, as everywhen in time, so everywhere in space, from the center of centers to the outermost rim of his mighty universe. This law is, as John beheld it, under the throne, the foundation of his moral government for all his morally accountable creatures. As the different States of our Union are ruled by the same Federal law from the capitol, so all worlds are ruled from his throne. Their Sabbath may not agree with ours in absolute time, but the principle is the same. He who discovered the plan of a flower discovered a plan which runs through all the floral kingdom. There are almost infinite variations, it is true, but still the plan is the same. So the plan of an animal runs through the whole animal kingdom, and on this fact is founded the science of comparative anatomy.

The Bible gives us, in simple language, the plan of God in creating worlds, and peopling them, and bringing them under his moral government. There may be variations in detail, but the principle is the same. Not even God himself could change that law and still be God.

The word "God" means good. God is the supreme, all-embracing Good. As in him are all the treasures of wisdom and knowledge, and all true learning is simply finding out him; so in him is all goodness, and all becoming good is simply becoming like him. The law is a record of God's goodness, of God's character; it, therefore, as David says, "is perfect, *as* he is perfect." When Solomon says, "Fear God, and keep his commandments; for this is the whole duty of man," it is only another way of saying that the whole duty of man is to be like his Maker. The life of God, as concerns moral principles, is written in that law, and was lived on earth by Jesus Christ.

As that law is God's will and God's character, even he cannot change it without changing himself. But as he includes all goodness now, he cannot change himself without changing to evil. But for God to become evil would be for him to cease to be God, for the word "God" means good. If God himself should change, and command what he has forbidden, and forbid what he has commanded, it would not change the underlying tendencies of those precepts to happiness or misery. It would change God into the embodiment of all evil, instead of all good. He would then be working for the misery of all his children, as now he is for their happiness and joy. It would then be true that God was hate, as now it is true that God is love.

The whole argument for the absolute stability and perpetuity of God's law rests on axiomatic truth. As it is utterly inconceivable to the human mind that there ever could be a world where, or a time when, two and two would be five instead of four, so it is unthinkable that there could be a world where, or a time when, these principles, if obeyed, would not lead to unity and happiness, and if disobeyed, to division, discord, misery, and strife. They rest upon love, and love never faileth. "Whether there be prophecies, they shall fail; whether there be tongues, they shall cease; whether there be knowledge, it shall vanish away;" but in the full dawning of that brighter day, before which the knowledge of the present shall vanish as the light of the candle before the rising sun, love shall be the rule of action for all; and these are the principles of love.

Notes:

1. Doctrine according to which Christians are freed by grace from the necessity of obeying the Mosaic Law.

XII

How Man Misunderstood His Maker

"No stream from its source
Flows seaward, how lonely soever its course,
But what some land is gladdened. No star ever rose
And set, without influence somewhere. Who knows
What earth needs from earth's lowliest creature? No life
Can be pure in its purpose and strong in its strife,
And all life not be purer and stronger thereby."

—Owen Meredith.

"Our echoes roll from soul to soul,
And grow forever and forever."

—Tennyson.

There are but two ways in life for men to travel, the one leading upward, with ever-increasing happiness, to God, the other downward through darkness to death. The first way is the way of God's law. We often hear men say when they have done anything peculiar, "Well, that is my way." This law is God's way. It is the way the angels walk, and that is why they are happy. This is the law of liberty. It defines the boundaries of the rights of every person. *Out of* this way, men have to suffer, not only for their own misdeeds, but for the sins of others also,—they not only sin, but are sinned against; *in* this way they can walk as brothers, in harmony and unity and joy.

There is not, and cannot be anywhere in the universe, any true happiness except that found in walking in this way. This is why God in "faithfulness and truth" counseled us all to walk in this way, and his counsels are "wonderful in wisdom, and excellent in working."

All this and more David saw when he said, "Blessed [or happy] are the undefiled in the way, who walk in the law of the Lord." No wonder that he prayed, as it is our privilege also to pray: "Teach me, O Lord, the way of thy statutes; and I shall keep it unto the end." "Make me to go in the path of thy commandments; for therein do I delight."

All turning aside from this way is following the counsels of the ungodly to sorrow and death. It was thus our first parents followed the counsels of Satan; and the race, which might have mounted, ere this, to unspeakable heights of glory and joy, has gone the downward way into misery and pain. It is not that God stands up above, and with arbitrary, vengeful hand pours down his wrath in misery upon the sinning; but it is the turning away of the simple that slays them. They simply "eat of the fruit of their own way," and this because they "would none" of God's counsels, and despised his reproofs.[1]

This is the one point that Satan has ever sought to hide from our eyes, that he might hasten us in the downward way. He has always beguiled us with the promise of pleasure, but the following of his counsels brought only pain. Then, pointing to the misery that resulted from our own actions, he said, "See, God is angry and vengeful, or he would not suffer this to come upon you."

It may be that our sorrow is not the result of our own sin, but of the sins of those around us. Man is not a solitary, but a social being. "None of us liveth to himself, and no man dieth to himself," Paul says; and in this there are depths of philosophy. The most selfish man lives to himself no more than the most unselfish; the difference is only in the nature of his influence on those around him. One life is a blessing and a benediction, the other a constant menace and curse. A stone thrown into a lake causes a series of constantly multiplying and enlarging circles. They may become invisible to us after a while, but if our eyesight were only perfect enough, we should discover that they ceased not till they rippled the waters against the farthermost shore.

The Bible often represents the mass of humanity as a lake or sea of waters. Every man's life is a bubble plunged into this ocean. For good or ill, for joy or sorrow, its influence rolls from soul to soul in ever-broadening circles, that cease not till the outermost marge[2] of human life is reached. We do not, we cannot, live and think and act alone. We are parts of a great whole, and our life affects all life.

Herein is the terrible injustice of evil. It was not Jesus alone that suffered, the innocent for the guilty. We all have to bear the sins and sorrows of those around us. God knew this when in love he pointed out the right way. Satan knew it when in malignant hatred of God he led men into the downward path. Now, watching, he discovers some poor innocent soul suffering in agony the result of the sins of those around him. The sorrowing heart seeks to rise in trembling faith to the consolation of the consciousness that God is love. But Satan whispers, "What have you done that you suffer so? How unjust it is in God to permit this? Surely he cannot love you, or this would not be." Thus Satan ever charges up to God the results that have come to men from rejecting God's counsel. No wonder James charges us: "Do not err, my beloved brethren. Every good gift and every perfect gift is from above, and cometh down from the Father of lights, with whom is no variableness, neither shadow of turning."

Satan has always been leading men to err here, and thus he has blinded them to God's love, and begotten within them hatred to God, instead of love. We have seen that love to God, the one Father, includes love to men, his children, and is therefore the fulfilling of the whole law. So hatred to God includes hatred to all his creatures, and is the breaking of the whole law. Through sin came sorrow and death upon all. Through sorrow and suffering came the idea that God is angry, and is punishing us unjustly, the innocent with the guilty.

Thus there came into the human heart hatred instead of love. But hatred leads to more sin,—in fact, to the breaking of every precept of the divine law. So, through hatred came more sin, and through sin more suffering, and through suffering more hatred, and through hatred more sin; and the world went on spinning down the dark circle of ever-increasing hatred, and increasing sin, and increasing misery, hateful and hating one another, every man's hand against his neighbor, the imaginations of their thoughts only evil, and evil continually. This is the cumulative downward tendency of sin.

Besides, through sin came an evil heredity. Men were born with the tendency to think wrong and do wrong. Through this came next an evil environment, exerting its influence for evil upon the child from his earliest conscious moments. Thus every deeper plunge of the soul into sin brought a worse heredity, and this brought a worse environment, and these brought more sin to lower still farther the standard of both the heredity and the environment. Ah, this was the downward way to death!

And Satan was all the while charging all this misery to God's forgetfulness of us, or to his hatred and wrath. What wonder men lost the knowledge of the true God! What wonder they lowered him ever downward to the embodiment of all evil, instead of all good, thus putting the devil in the place of God! And so they did, for all paganism was in part devil-worship. Paul says, "The things which the Gentiles sacrifice, they sacrifice to devils, and not to God." Thus men were estranged from God. Not that God ceased to love them, but they ceased to love God; and ceasing to love the one Father, they ceased to love one another. Sin built up a high wall, or partition, between man and God, and between man and man.

God does not need to be reconciled to man, for, like the mother's love, his love ever follows us, even when we are in the downward way, seeking to bring us back to him. But man needs to be reconciled to God. In some way there must be an atonement made. Not that God's wrath must be satisfied, so that he will look with favor upon offending man, but that God's love must be so manifest, in spite of the existence of suffering and sin, that men will turn their hearts toward him, as the flower toward the sun. The power of the sun to warm the earth after the night of storm is its power to shine away the mists and the darkness, so that men may behold its glorious face. So the power of God to warm the hard, cold hearts of men into new love and life is his power to shine away the almost impenetrable mist and darkness that sin has cast around his character, so that men may see him as he is, and know that God is love.

This is the work of Christ, the Sun of Righteousness. How he accomplishes it I shall seek to show in succeeding chapters. Let us praise him here, that his love forsook us not when we were wandering from him; but even while we were dead in sins, for his great love wherewith he loved us, he quickened us together with Christ, that by this manifestation of his unmerited favor we might be saved.

"*God so loved the world*." The word "world" here is cosmos, which means order, harmony, arrangement. But the world was out of order, and out of harmony, almost a chaos instead of a cosmos. God created the world for his pleasure, for his glory; but we had all sinned and come short of the glory of God. His high ideal was still unrealized in us. Anything short of divine love would have left us to our fate,—the hopeless destruction of the culminating downward tendencies of misery and sin.

Here God's love looked at us, not as we were, but as we were capable of becoming. He beheld us, not in the darkness of the present sin, but in the glorious light of the possible future. Underneath the chaos he beheld the cosmos,—every creature in blessed unity saying, "Blessing, and honor, and glory, and power, be unto Him that sitteth upon the throne, and unto the Lamb forever and ever." His love clung to us still, and gave his Son to bring out this possibility within us. Of this Paul speaks when he says, "I reckon that the sufferings of this present time are not worthy to be compared with the glory which shall be revealed in us."

What is this love of God but the father and mother love that ever follows the wayward child in all his wanderings,—follows him though the world has forsaken him and cast him off, ever believing in some possible future for him that the world sees not, and ever seeking, with almost infinite love and longing, to bring out that possible within him? This is what God means when he says, The mother may forget her child, but I will not forget you.

How comforting to know that he looks at us now ever thus, beholding not our sins and the chaos of human passions and of selfishness that reigns within, but beholding still the ideal beauty of character for which he made us, and which he ever seeks to bring out within us! Ah! this is love, for God is love! As he said to the storm-tossed sea, so to the passion-tossed soul Jesus waits, and waits in love, to say, "Peace, be still,"—only waits the lifted eye of faith and trust that cries, "Master, carest thou not that we perish?"

Notes:

1. Prov. 1:29–33.
2. Margin.

XIII

The Atonement

"For this cause I bow my knees unto the Father of our Lord Jesus Christ, of whom the whole family in heaven and earth is named."

—Paul

The word "atonement" means *at-one-ment.* Sin had brought misery, and misery had brought a misunderstanding of God's character. Thus men had come to hate God instead of loving him; and hating him, the one Father, men also hated man, their brother. Thus, instead of the one family and the one Father, men were separated from God and from each other, and held apart by hatred and selfishness. There must be an atonement.

An atonement can be made only by God revealing his love, in spite of sin and sorrow, so that men's hearts will be touched to tenderness; and they, being delivered from Satan's delusions, may see how fully and terribly they have misunderstood the divine One, and so done despite the Spirit of his grace. Thus they may be led, as returning brethren, to come back to the Father's house in blissful unity.

The atonement is not to appease God's wrath, so that man dare come to him, but it is to reveal his love, so that they will come to him. It was not Christ reconciling God unto the world, but God in Christ reconciling the world unto himself. It is nowhere said that God needed to be reconciled unto us; he says, "I have not forsaken you, but you have forsaken me." And Paul says, "I beseech you in Christ's stead, Be ye reconciled to God." It was this question that needed to be answered: How can it be that God is our Father, and that he is love, when we suffer so much, and oftentimes so unjustly, and yet no voice breaks the silence, no Father's touch soothes our sorrow? The question was to be answered by God, through Christ, breaking the silence, and through him healing the sick, and raising the dead, prophetic of the time when, Satan's power being broken, all tears shall be wiped away.

Thus it was revealed that misery was not God's will, the result of his wrath, but that it was the devil's will, the result of sin. Christ's whole life, from Bethlehem's manger to Calvary's cross, was a life of untarnished, unadulterated love. But who was Christ? The word means "anointed." He was the anointed of God, anointed with God's Spirit to live God's life on earth. Said the angel: "They shall call his name Emanuel, which being interpreted is, GOD WITH US."

Ah, yes! There had been gods enough before Jesus came to reveal to a lost world the knowledge of the Father. In Egypt it was said at one time that it was easier to find a god than a man, so numerous were they. The trouble was, none of them was "our Father." They were none of them "with us." They were all gods afar off in the distant and in the dim, and none of them loved the human soul. There were gods of war, and gods of storm, and gods of lust, and theft, and drunken revelings, till every base and angry passion of the lost soul was deified and worshiped, to drag the soul farther down into sin and resultant misery. There was a god in the clouds to shoot forth the arrows of the angry lightnings; a god in the ocean to toss the waves on high, and wreck the ships freighted with human life; a god in the earth to make it tremble with terror, and pour forth the lava from the mountain top, desolating the cities at its base; a god everywhere for wrath and destruction; a god everywhere whose wrath must be appeased by some bloody sacrifice; a god everywhere, but always too far away to be reached by the prayers of trembling faith, surging up from suffering souls.

But when Jesus came, he was God with us,—with us in sorrow, for he was a man of sorrows and acquainted with grief; with us in joy, for he, too, rejoiced at the wedding feast; with us in childhood, for he was a child, and even the child's timid prayer can reach his heart; with us in youth, for he knows all its slippery paths, all its haunting fears, that so silently take the place of the fleeting phantoms of its high ideals, and high hopes unrealized; with us in poverty, for he had not where to lay his head; with us in work and weariness, for he was a carpenter, and the son of a carpenter;

with us in persecution, for he was led as a lamb to the slaughter; with us in the sad hour of final parting from the loved ones, for did he not on the cross say to John, "Behold thy mother"? with us when our faith almost fails, for did not he, too, say in anguish of spirit, "My God, my God, why hast thou forsaken me?" with us in the dark valley of death, for he "likewise took part of the same; that through death he might destroy him that had the power of death, that is, the devil." Ah, yes! he was "Emanuel, which being interpreted is, God with us."

How the devil's falsehoods flee as we behold God revealed in Jesus Christ! How the estranged soul comes back to its native home, and becomes *at one* with God! "Yea, the sparrow hath found a house, and the swallow a nest for herself, where she may lay her young, even thine altars, O Lord of hosts, my King, and my God." What wonder that the newly created Paul preached to the Athenian idolaters the truth that God is not far from every one of us! He found that out on the journey to Damascus, when the light shone around him, and a voice said, "Saul, Saul, why persecutest thou me?"

Glimmerings of this same glorious truth had been given the faithful in all the past. It was thus that Enoch had walked with God. It was this that Jacob learned that night in Bethel. Was there ever a time when God *seemed* farther away from any human soul than from Jacob that night? Driven away from home on account of his own and his mother's sin, a weary wanderer in the wilderness, no house in sight, the night thickening around, and only a stone for a pillow, the damp earth underneath, and apparently only the stars for watchers overhead,—ah! if there was ever a time when God *seemed* far away, and the heart was lonely and desolate, and the future all unknown, it was then. But God revealed even to the sinful Jacob the truth that from every human soul there is a ladder reaching to heaven, and that on it the angels of God are ascending and descending, and that from the top our Father looks lovingly down on his child with promise and benediction. We, too, from the hour of deepest darkness may wake to know that "this is none other but the house of God. and this is the gate of heaven."

It was this, too, which Job saw when, amid his afflictions, property consumed, health gone, forsaken by friends, even his wife urging him to curse God and die, yet with magnificent faith, that showed how near God was to his soul in spite of all the misfortunes of life, he said: "I know that my Redeemer liveth, and that he shall stand at the latter day upon the earth; and though after my skin worms destroy this body, yet in my flesh shall I see God."

These people, like Abraham, saw beforehand Christ's day, and, seeing it, were made glad. In Christ thus was God's love revealed in spite of the sorrow that sin has brought,—a love that willingly stooped to bear our sins and share our sorrows, that he might bring us to God; a love that even now on the darkest storm cloud paints the bow of promise, and that shall yet make the crooked straight, and the rough places plain, so that all flesh shall see his glory.

Truly, "he is our peace, who hath made both one, and hath broken down the middle wall of partition between us," so that we are no longer "strangers and foreigners, but fellow citizens with the saints, and of the household of God." He hath made the at-one-ment, having reconciled us to God, so that, through him, man with man and man with God shall yet be brought into blissful unity. And not only man with man and man with God, but in the love of God as revealed in Jesus Christ shall all intelligent, morally accountable creatures find their rallying-point, their rest, and universal brotherhood of being, "that in the dispensation of the fullness of times he might gather together in one all things in Christ, both which are in heaven, and which are on earth; even in him, in whom also we have obtained an inheritance."

It is the goodness of God that leads us back to the Father's house in repentance. This goodness is revealed through Christ; so "him hath God exalted. . . to be a Prince and a Saviour, for to give repentance to Israel, and forgiveness of sins."

The theological world resolves itself into two great schools. The first of these is represented by so-called orthodoxy, the last, by Unitarianism.[1] The first one of these schools is always talking about the death of Christ; the last, about his life.

Now it is impossible to dwell too much upon the death of Christ; and it is also impossible to linger too lovingly over the memory of his life, but the two should not be separated in the thought. Nothing earthly is more capable of inspiring the soul and lifting it to noble endeavor than the self-sacrificing, heroic death of the merely human hero; but that death is inspiring, becomes heroic in fact, only when taken in connection with the life,—with the circumstances which led to the death. So with the death of the divine Son of God; it is not the death only, but the life also, for Paul says, "If, when we were enemies, we were reconciled to God by the death of his Son, much more, being reconciled, we shall be saved by his life."

The death of Christ becomes significant only when taken in connection with his life of self-sacrifice, which led to and was the cause of his death. Only thus does the death have power to reveal God's love so as to reconcile us to him; and it was during that life that God wove in him that perfect, spotless robe of his righteousness which, by faith, is first attributed to us and then wrought out in us, thus covering and subduing all our sins. Let us then ever exalt the life and death of the Son of God as the world's hope of salvation. It was these that made the atonement; and there is "none other name under heaven given among men, whereby we must be saved."

The first of these theological schools, neglecting almost entirely and failing to understand the humanity of Christ, is ever exclaiming, "*Ecce Deus!*" (Behold the God); while the last, denying the divinity of Christ, takes up the cry, "*Ecce homo!*" (Behold the man.) It seems to the author that both of these make a grave, if not fatal mistake.

With reference to the first I would say, God is love. Love, and therefore God, is most revealed in Jesus Christ when we remember that in him, for our good, divinity actually took upon itself humanity, with all its weakness and weariness, with all its passions, and loves, and longings, and with all its temptations. In fact, it is only thus that Christ reveals God, and is himself divine, for God is love.

On the other hand, if Jesus was only human, and not the divine Son, how did it come that his life so transcends all other lives ever lived in this world, towering so above all men of his time and of all other times, as to stand alone, the one center of type and memorial, of prophecy and history, of hope and faith, for past and coming ages? If only human, how does it reveal other than the human? how does it so reveal God as to bring the world back to him? If only human, what can it do for the human race, only to lift, it may be, the tide of their aspirations and longings a little higher without increasing the power for a possible realization? This were but to increase their misery by taunting them with impossibilities. It were but to hold above them the apple of life, only keeping it ever beyond their grasp. Ah, no! this is not like God. Either of these extremes is fatal.

We need simply to believe the Bible record of the incarnation. We cannot understand it. What have we yet understood of the mystery of even vegetable and animal life? Here reason fails, and the most blatant science stands dumb, and yet here we believe and know. Why should we wonder that the divine life in Christ, and through him in us, should be a mystery; and why refuse to believe in it because it is a mystery? What does the incarnation mean?—Simply this, that God was in Christ, reconciling the world unto himself; that Jesus was divine, and yet human, perfect God and perfect man, Son of God and Son of man; that with the divine arm he might grasp the throne of the Infinite, while with the human arm he encircles humanity, with all its woes and needs, with all its hungerings and heartaches, and encircles it to lift it up, to unite it with God, thus making the atonement.

This, I repeat, like the mystery of the lower life, may be beyond our reasonings, but it is not unreasonable, for it is like God; for this is love, and "God is love."

Notes:

1. Unitarianism: 1) One who believes that the deity exists only in one person. 2) A member of a denomination that stresses individual freedom of belief, the free use of reason in religion, a united world community, and liberal social action.

XIV

The Atonement Vicarious

"Surely he hath borne our griefs, and carried our sorrows; yet we did esteem him stricken, smitten of God, and afflicted. But he was wounded for our transgressions, he was bruised for our iniquities: the chastisement of our peace was upon him; and with his stripes we are healed."

—Isa. 53:4, 5

After reading the last chapter, some conscientious but timid soul may ask, "Is not this denying the vicarious atonement?" I answer, No; a thousand times no. It is only lifting and broadening and enlarging our conception of the vicarious atonement, and bringing it into harmony with what we know of God's character, as revealed in his work and his word. Jesus is still the world's only Saviour. Both in life and in death he suffered vicariously, bearing our griefs and carrying our sorrows,—"suffering the Just for the unjust, that he might bring us to God," that is, that he might make an atonement.

Christ's death was not the result of an outpouring of the Father's wrath; it was the result of the world's violation of the Father's law of love. His death was simply the climax of his life. In every day's labor of love he had been giving his life, his very heart and soul, to uplift and redeem humanity; but the hearts of men were so cold and hard through sin that they knew it not. On Calvary he completed the gift, while the world mocked at the foot of the cross. He lived a perfectly unselfish life, in a world of sin and selfishness; and the world hated him because his life showed the selfishness and hypocrisy of its own. Paul said that if he preached circumcision, he would escape persecution, for then would the offense of the cross cease. So with Jesus; if he had turned to the right or the left from the straight line of truth, he might have escaped the crucifixion.

The devil and wicked men hate truth, not error; nevertheless, it is the truth only that can save men. Jesus kept this ever in mind, and, constantly saying, "Not my will, but thine be done," he was ever loyal to the truth, and his life led to his death; the cross was at the end of the avenue of self-sacrifice. In all this he was only bearing our griefs and carrying our sorrows. His life and death were like those of the prophets before him and the apostles after him, only that in him the ideal was reached and realized. Stephen said to the Jews: "Ye stiff-necked and uncircumcised in heart and ears, ye do always resist the Holy Ghost; as your fathers did, so do ye. Which of the prophets have not your fathers persecuted? and they have slain them which showed before of the coming of the Just One; of whom ye have been now the betrayers and murderers." Thus, as Jesus in his life was in all things made like unto his brethren, so in his death he is classed with the faithful who had gone before, and those who should come after.

In the parable (Matt. 21:33-41), the householder sent to his vineyard servant after servant; one they beat, another they killed, and another they stoned. Finally, he sent his own son, and him also they treated likewise, and slew him. As Jesus beheld the enormity of their past guilt, and saw what the church was to do in the future, in anguish of spirit he exclaimed: "O Jerusalem, Jerusalem, thou that killest the prophets, and stonest them which are sent unto thee, how often would I have gathered thy children together, even as a hen gathereth her chickens under her wings, and ye would not!" It is thus every age has persecuted its prophets and apostles, leaving posterity to build their sepulchers and do them honor.

All the apostles save one suffered martyrdom, and tradition says of him that he was miraculously delivered. When Paul was suffering the persecution and imprisonment that preceded his crucifixion, he wrote of himself to the Colossian brethren thus: "I Paul . . . now rejoice in my sufferings for you, and fill up that which is behind of the afflictions of Christ in my flesh for his body's sake, which is the church." When he was about to be crucified, he said, "I am now ready to be offered."

Ah, yes! we make a great mistake when we separate between the life and the death of Christ, or the life and the death of the Christian, as if they were two different things. We lose the consolation of the fact that as he was "made perfect through suffering," so we, through this same suffering, are made one with him. As he was the mystery of God, God manifest in the flesh, so Paul says, "The riches of the glory of this mystery . . . is Christ in you, the hope of glory." (Compare 1 Tim. 3:16 with Col. 1:27.)

Jesus was innocent. He suffered only for the sins of others. All his grief was bearing *our* griefs and carrying *our* sorrows, and this he did that he might bring us to God. We, unlike Jesus, have all sinned, and we suffer for our own sins and bear our own griefs; but, besides this and beyond this, we, like him, suffer for the sins and bear the griefs of others. We have not only sinned, but we have been sinned against.

O weary, waiting, anguished soul, has thy life been blighted, and thine heart been made desolate by that which was not thy fault? Have the bright hopes of a buoyant youth faded and fallen like the autumn leaves, finding a grave in thy longing, lonely heart; and all because another was false when thou didst believe him true? Have fortune and friends forsaken thee because of the sin of another? Art thou persecuted and despised because the world hates what God and thou dost love? Hast thou through all this been tempted to doubt the justice and love of the Divine One? This is not the injustice of God. This is the injustice of sin, the inevitable, unavoidable result of the world's sin. Even Jesus, the Father's own and only begotten Son, when in the world, suffered all this.

Dost thou doubt God's love for thee because of this? It is but to doubt God's love for him. Rather remember that in this thou, if thou trust him, art made one with him, for "all things work together for good to them that love God." He was led "as a lamb to slaughter, and as a sheep before her shearers is dumb," so he opened not his mouth. Remember if thou too bearest it patiently, and for him, thy life also, with his, is presented a living sacrifice, holy and acceptable, a part of the world's great sacrifice for sin. Also remember that in this thy life of patient love may reach some other life and turn it to him for redemption, so that thou too, by and by, mayest enter into his joy. Remembering this, does not thine heart beat high with new comfort and hope, and new courage to go bravely on and meet life's conflict?

But, says one, if this is the nature of Christ's sacrifice, a living sacrifice as well as a dying one, why is the blood always the symbol of that sacrifice? and why is it said that without the shedding of blood there is no remission?

Ah, in this there are depths of meaning! It is because Jesus was true unto the death. With him there was no flinching, no turning aside, though he beheld the cross at the end of the journey. He said, "Father, not my will, but thine be done." His death has meaning only when taken as one with his life, and his life takes on new glory when thus we behold it, as leading to his death.

He requires us to live that life. He says, "If ye love father or mother, or houses, or lands, or any earthly treasure, even your own life, more than me, ye are not worthy of me." If anything, even the cross at the end of the pathway we tread, will turn us aside from the way, we are not his; and if we are not his, there is no remission. Nothing but the blood could signify a sacrifice so complete.

Then it is not in death only that the life's blood is given. It was Paul who spoke of "always bearing about in the body the dying of the Lord Jesus, that the life also of Jesus might be made manifest in our body." It can be manifest in no other way. The heart that is broadened and made tender through suffering, till, like his, it takes in humanity with all its needs and all its longings, giving unasked sympathy and helpfulness to all,—this heart knows what it is to give its life-blood daily, to die daily, that the life of Christ may be manifest in it. There are times when it takes more courage and true heroism to live, and live right, than to die. The heart, after storm and struggle are over, beats quietly toward the close. Yes, Carlyle well says, "My brother, the brave man has to give his life away. Give it, I advise thee; thou dost not expect to sell thy life in any adequate manner? The 'wages' of every noble work do yet lie in heaven or else nowhere." It is a daily giving of the life, such as only the shedding of the life's blood can signify. This is Christianity.

And are not His experiences ours? Behold him at the baptism in Jordan. The Spirit descends like a dove upon him, and the voice is heard saying, "This is my beloved Son, in whom I am well pleased." Surely, we would have said, with such a beginning of his mission, there is before him only a life of triumph and joy. But it was from this that he was led of the Spirit into the wilderness, to be tempted of the devil.

Do we not remember the joy of our conversion, when we consecrated ourselves to him, and his sweet forgiveness came into our hearts? Did not the Spirit descend, and was not the Father's voice heard, perhaps for the first time, saying to our happy souls, "This is my beloved son, in whom I am well pleased"? How we almost fancied that the struggle was over and the victory gained! Ah! but have we not since then too often found life's pathway a desert, doleful and demon-peopled, in which we have wandered hungry and weary? Was it not at the moment when our strength had well-nigh failed that the devil forsook us at some promise of the written word, and some kind angel came and ministered unto us?

Then life has had its ordinary days of service, when from sun to sun we have worked in His vineyard. There was the morning's freshness, and the noontide heat, and the evening's weariness. There have been nights of watching and praying alone on some moonlit mountain side. There have been days of work that seemed to bring no passing reward; and which of us have not wept and wondered that, of the ten that were healed by our love and care, the nine came not back to render due meed[1] of thanks?

Perhaps we have felt at times that we too had not where to lay our head; but which of us has not had his Bethany home, where he might rest for a time, and find loving, grateful ministration, where the winds of the world might blow without, but they touch us not there? We, too, have had times when with Him we have been transfigured on faith's mountain summit. For the time we have beheld ourselves, not as we were, but as we were capable of becoming. The world, with its rush, and roar, and mad ambitions, and discordant voices, was far below. Some friend might be near who knew us not, or only half knew, but we were alone with Him. The Father's voice again spake and owned us as his, and bright visions of meeting with glorified forms came to speak of the future kingdom where we too shall reign with him. Have we not, or may we not, from this mountain summit come down to find our Gethsemane and Calvary; the struggle to say, "Thy will be done;" the doubt that said in anguish, "My God, my God, why hast thou forsaken me?"—happy if at last the unshaken, triumphant faith, that, amid a darkened sun and angry lightning's flash and rending rocks, said: "It is finished," "Father, into thy hands I commend my spirit."

May we not from his life learn that God's love is the one unvarying quantity through all these fears and fluctuations, ever the same, from everlasting to everlasting? May we not rejoice that through these experiences we can be one with Jesus here, and one with him hereafter? It was all this that Paul saw when he said: "Not only so, but we glory in tribulations also; knowing that tribulation worketh patience; and patience, experience; and experience, hope; and hope maketh not ashamed; because the love of God is shed abroad in our hearts."

Notes:

1. A fitting return or recompense.

XV

Miracles and Their Meaning

"The Father that dwelleth in me, he doeth the works."

—Jesus

When it is said that in the incarnation the Son of God actually became the Son of man, giving us not only his glory and honor, but his power as well, and taking in return only our poverty and weakness, it is often asked, "What about miracles? do they not prove that Jesus had, *in himself*, while here, the divine creative power?" I answer, No;—

1. Because, if they prove this of Jesus, they prove the same for all the apostles. Did not they also heal the sick, and even raise the dead? Were not handkerchiefs taken from their persons potent to heal disease? Did not Jesus say to his church in reference to his works, "The works that I do shall ye do also; and greater works than these shall ye do; because I go to my Father"?

2. Because, if that divine power was inherent in him while here, he was not "in all things made like unto his brethren," and he could not have been "tempted in all points like as we are," so as to be "touched with the feeling of our infirmities."

3. If he had this power in himself while here, why did he spend nights in patient prayer, pleading for strength and deliverance? Why, when tempted of the devil, instead of meeting Satan with direct power and vanquishing him, did he resort, as we have to do, to the promises of the written word to make Satan flee? Why, when his strength failed, was it necessary for angels to come and minister unto him?
4. Why does he never claim the power as his own, but, instead, always give the glory to the Father, as at the grave of Lazarus, where he said: "Father, I thank thee that thou hast heard me. And I knew that thou hearest me always; but because of the people which stand by I said it, that they may believe that thou hast sent me"? Why does he not say, "If I by my own power cast out devils," instead of, "If I cast out devils by the Spirit of God, then the kingdom of God is come unto you"? Why is it said that it was through the eternal Spirit that he offered himself without spot for us?
5. Why does Jesus emphatically say, "I can of mine own self do nothing," "the Father that dwelleth in me, he doeth the works"?

All this is sufficient to show that Jesus, while here, was of himself actually weak and powerless, like one of us. His life is not an evidence of what God could do himself if here in person and power. The world needs no new evidence of that. The earth, with its green, grassy carpet under our feet, and the universe of suns and worlds around us, and held suspended in space over our heads, is certainly present and sufficient proof of that. Jesus' life is an evidence of what God can do, and of what he is willing to do, by his Spirit, working through human weakness. He was God manifest in the flesh. Forget this, and imagine that Christ himself had inherent power, more than human, while here, and you have robbed his whole life of its lesson of meaning and helpfulness for us.

The world, lost in sin and separated from God, needed more than to have God revealed, and the right way to him pointed out. This alone would have left them longing but impotent, as was Paul when he said, "O wretched man that I am! who shall deliver me from the body of this death?" Men needed, also, to have the source of power presented, by which they could be enabled to walk in this highway of holiness.

This source of power must be revealed before the atonement could be made; for men, to be made one with God and one with each other, must be enabled, in spite of sin and the inherent hereditary weakness of sin, to walk this upward way. So, "what the law could not do, in that it was weak through the flesh, God sending his own Son in the likeness of sinful flesh, and for sin, condemned sin in the flesh; that the righteousness of the law might be fulfilled in us, who walk not after the flesh, but after the "Spirit."[1] The law was weak to condemn man because it could not give the weakened flesh power to keep it. Christ revealed the power of God to keep that law in us, if we yield ourselves to the control of his Spirit.

This is the meaning of every miracle, and of Christ's whole life of spotless purity, which was itself the greatest miracle of all. Jesus emptied himself. He gave up his own will, his own way, his own power, his own words; and God willed in him, and worked in him, and spoke through him. So intimate was this union that Jesus said, "I and my Father are one;" "he that hath seen me hath seen the Father."

But just as God wrought through him, so Jesus waits to work through us. Paul says, "For by one Spirit are we all baptized into one body." Now baptism means death and burial. When we present our bodies a living and daily dying sacrifice, as did Jesus; when our independent wills die, so that in all the church there is but one mind, one controlling power, then the atonement will be complete, then the church will indeed be one body with Christ, then will Christ will and work in us to do of his good pleasure, as the Father did in him. For, I repeat, if the mystery of God was God manifest in Christ's flesh, Paul says the riches of the glory of that mystery for you and me is, "Christ in us the hope of glory." Then it will not be merely Christ in the Father, and the Father in Christ, so that these two are one, but Jesus says, "At that day ye shall know that I am in my Father, and *ye in me, and I in you.*" When this is true, then, indeed, is the atonement complete.

Every miracle of Christ is an evidence of the power of the divine love to work in us, and lift us to him. How often we have looked upon them as mere manifestations of physical force, given to make the world look and wonder, and almost compel its belief! Ah, no, this was not the meaning! If it was, why did Jesus so often, after his greatest miracles, say to the one healed, "See thou tell no man"? Why not rather say, "Publish it abroad everywhere, that you may advertise to the world that I am the Messiah"?

The fact is, the miracle separated from the motive of love which was back of it,—the miracle, considered merely as a miracle,—was no evidence of Messiahship at all. Satan always has his miracles, but they have no love in them, and so no spiritual power for good. By these miracles, as in the time of Moses, he always resists the truth. He is to work in the last days with all power, and signs, and lying wonders, and all deceivableness of unrighteousness in them that perish. When he works thus, Jesus himself calls him a false christ, with power to deceive all but the very elect.

Why has he no power to deceive the elect?—Because they are kept by the power of God through faith unto salvation; because they have learned that God is love, and that a miracle, to be any evidence of the divine mission and divine power of the worker, must be such a miracle as manifests only love's power. Such were the miracles of Jesus. Every one was wrought for love's sake; not to exhibit mere physical power, not to gain popularity or fame, but rather to reveal to the world the power of the divine love, which is the only power that can heal the soul as well as the body, and unite it to him.

One day a blind man called after Jesus, saying, "Thou Son of David, have mercy on me!" He who had beheld all the glory of heaven, and gazed even from within on the beauty of the rainbow that surrounds the throne; he who even here in this world, cursed by sin, felt his sensitive soul thrill with pleasure at every lingering remnant of the former grandeur, drawing lessons of hope and cheer from raven and sparrow, and the spotless purity of the lily's white leaf,—he felt his heart touched to tenderest sympathy for this man, locked up in perpetual darkness, and, strong in love's power through faith, he touched his eyes, and they were healed. Then straightway he charged him to tell no man. There was no desire for a public recognition. It was enough for Love to know that joy had been given and gratefully received.

One day they brought to him a deaf man, and he led him aside from the multitude. And he who participated when the morning stars sang together, and all the sons of God shouted for joy; he who had listened to the majestic symphonies of the angel choirs; he who even here rejoiced in every tone of nature's music, and every warbled song of praise,—he felt his soul thrill with love's longing for that man locked up in perpetual silence, and he healed him, that he might hear and join the universal psalm of praise. But again he charged him that he should tell no man.

He who had fasted forty days, and hungered, refused to send the hungry multitude away, lest they faint on the road. Even at the grave of Lazarus, where such wonderful power was manifest, it is not recorded that at the time the people were so much astonished at the mere power itself; that came afterward, when the sweet, subduing influence of the moment had passed; but it is recorded that there, as Jesus wept, they said, "Behold how he loved him!" *Behold how he loved him!* Yes, this is the meaning of Christ's miracles. They reveal the divine love, which thrills with sympathy for human needs and human heartaches, and is therefore powerful for our healing.

"God is love." The miracles of Jesus revealed love; they therefore revealed God, and proclaimed Jesus the Messiah, the Anointed of God. And why did Jesus weep?—He loved Lazarus. He loved Mary and Martha, now bereaved. He loved the Bethany home, where he, too, had rested when weary, and the circle of whose loving hearts was now broken. But, more than this, this was an image to him of all the grief that death had brought into the world; this family, an image of other families; and this sad parting with the loved one, an image of all such sad separations. His heart took in a hungry, weary humanity, waiting here in grief and tears for the dawning of a better day.

Ah, sad and suffering soul, separated from those thou lovest, the heart's tendrils all torn and bare and bleeding, dost thou fancy no eye sees thy sorrow, that no heart beats responsive to thy grief? Heaven itself has known the sorrow of parting from its Lord, and all the pearly portals of those mansions of the skies, so wont to ring to seraphs' song, were hushed and draped in mourning. And somewhere, we know, though their tears may not reach this earth, the angels still weep over the sadness of our parting hours. And not only the angels, but in that weeping at the tomb of Lazarus, Jesus wept for us all. He revealed to us God, and both Father and Son change not, but are the same yesterday, and today, and forever. They stoop to oneness with us, even now, in our sorrow, that we may be lifted to oneness with them in their joy. It is thus that Jesus stooped to conquer sin and make the atonement. This is love, for God is love.

Notes:

1. Rom. 8:3, 4.

XVI

The Sacrifice of Christ Honors God's Law

"Open thou mine eyes, that I may behold wondrous things out of thy law."

—Ps. 119:18

Satan has always said that God's law was arbitrary and unjust, and his government tyrannical. By this means he seeks to justify his secession from that government, and his attempt to exalt his own throne above the stars of God.

In past chapters we have endeavored to show that, notwithstanding Satan's cavils,[1] the law is a divine revelation of infinite, unchanging love. It is our object in this chapter to show how in the sacrifice of Christ the law of God was exalted, and its love revealed, and yet the transgressor mercifully pardoned, so that sinful man could be made one with God.

Paul says, "Do we then make void the law through faith?" This is precisely what many modern theologians affirm. Such should hear Paul's answer: "God forbid; yea, we establish the law" (through faith, understood).[2] How is it we establish God's law when we have faith in Christ? Let us ask another question, Why did God not pardon the sinner without the sacrifice of Christ? Was it because he did not love man sufficiently?—Ah, no!

God is revealed through Jesus Christ. Christ says, "I and my Father are one." At the crucifixion, both the expression of the divine love and the revelation of the world's depths of defiant sin came to the climax. But even there Jesus, dying on the cross while the unrepentant world scoffed at its feet, poured forth his soul's longings for man in these words, "Father, forgive them; for they know not what they do."

Thus is revealed how God feels even toward an unrepentant world. He longs to forgive them. Why does he not do it?—Such an act would ignore his law and set it at naught, thus leading others to thoughtlessly violate it. But the violation of that law brings as an unavoidable result misery and death. No forgiveness that could not remove these would be worth having. A forgiveness that led more men into them would be a curse rather than a blessing. Every good father has at times felt a desire to grant his child some present pleasure, but has been compelled to forbear, for fear of future pain.

Paul says of Christ: "In whom we have redemption through his blood, the forgiveness of sins, according to the riches of his grace, wherein he hath abounded toward us in all wisdom and prudence." This plainly shows that God's love and favor, had God been unwise, might have abounded toward us in an imprudent way; but through Jesus they were so prudently manifest that the sinner may have pardon and peace, and yet not be led thereby to regard sin lightly; yea, more, he may have pardon and peace, and yet the law be so exalted and magnified that multitudes will be led back to their allegiance.

If the governor of a State should indiscriminately pardon all offenses against the law, it would absolutely abolish all restraint of law. The motive in his mind might be love, but that love would be so unwisely and imprudently manifested that it would lead to anarchy and misery. The same is true of the Governor of the universe. His love and his wisdom are one. His pardoning power must be so exercised in "wisdom and prudence" as to lead men to unity and joy, and not to anarchy and misery, else it is not love.

When Fort Sumter was fired upon, if in a sickly sentimentality the United States had said, "Now we do not want to hurt these men; we will let them all go free, rather than punish them and cause misery to their families," our laws, our government, would have been dishonored and disgraced. Men would have said, "The Americans have no respect for their laws; they will not defend their government." Our unity would have been lost. Other nations would have come in each for his share of our territory, and untold misery and slavery and death would have been the result.

Instead of this, we sent forth our noblest sons. They shed their life's blood, they gave themselves a living and dying sacrifice to put down the rebellion. When the rebellion was put down, and the seceders surrendered, then we manifested our disposition to pardon. We pardoned every one who would lay down his arms. Even leaders in that rebellion were freely forgiven. This we could do now, and no one would say that we did not respect our laws. This we could do now, and not have it tend to more misery.[3]

Sin is secession from the government of God. Satan seceded, and sought to exalt his throne above that of God. Sinners are those who have joined themselves to Satan's forces in this secession. God, in infinite love, sends his own and only Son to put down the rebellion. He cannot pardon those who are still in rebellion, for this would but justify the rebellion and dishonor the law, and so perpetuate and multiply the misery. But through Jesus this rebellion is finally to be put down entirely. "The seed of the woman shall bruise the serpent's head." O'er every hilltop of earth and heaven, where for a short time there has waved the black standard of the man of sin, there shall forever float the white pennon of the Prince of Peace.

Every one who lays down his arms and surrenders his opposing will to God has the promise of pardon. This pardon God can grant, and not dishonor his law. Yea, more, it is through this pardon that the mercy and love of God's law and government are revealed,—a love that only commanded the right way, not to be arbitrary and domineering, but that men might be happy,—a love that when men repent of the wrong, and turn back their hearts toward the broken law, is ever willing to forgive the past and give power for future obedience. It is thus that God can be just, and still the justifier of those who believe on Jesus.[4] It is thus that faith in Jesus exalts the law of God to the highest heavens, and establishes it forever.

The cross of Calvary, to the whole universe of intelligent beings, is the greatest demonstration that ever has been or ever can be given that God's law is eternal and universal, and yet that his love is infinite; reaching down with tender, fatherly longing to lift up the lowest transgressor. In fact, his love is his law, and the law is unchangeable because his love is from everlasting to everlasting. When men behold this, they are led to repent of past transgressions, and to pray for power for future obedience. It is thus that Christ is exalted to be a Prince and a Saviour, to give repentance to Israel and forgiveness of sins.[5] It is thus that the atonement is made, and rebellious men are led back into unity with God and with one another.

The life and death of Jesus—there it stands and will stand throughout eternal ages, an unanswerable argument to all intelligent beings of God's unspeakable love, that first found expression in the law, and then, when men had violated that law, was more fully revealed through Christ; a divine, unanswerable argument to prove that—

1. If men suffer, it may not be because they are personally guilty, but because of the sins of others. Jesus also suffered, the just for the unjust.
2. It is not because God is angry with us, or hates us, that we suffer; for he loved Jesus, his only begotten Son, yet Jesus suffered more than we all.
3. All the misery of the world is the result of the world's violation of God's law of love, the keeping of which is the only possible way intelligent beings can be happy. Misery is, therefore, not only not an evidence of the Father's forgetfulness or hatred, but a direct, unanswerable proof of that fatherly, solicitous love which in the law said, "Thou shalt not, my son, thou shalt not."
4. The only way out of this pit of darkness into which we have fallen is to repent of sin and yield our hearts to keep the divine law. We can then be forgiven without God's ignoring this law, and then God can give us power, as he did Jesus, to condemn sin in the flesh, and he, by his Spirit, can fulfill the righteousness of the law in us.
5. When this is done, we must not look for freedom from sorrow in this world, for we, with him, shall bear the sins and sorrows of others; but we may look for the rest that remaineth for the people of God,—for the great eternity where all the wrongs of earth shall be righted, and where what is dark here shall be light in heaven. With Job we say, "I know that my Redeemer liveth," and with David, "I shall be satisfied when I awake with thy likeness." With all the innumerable company we shall reckon ourselves pilgrims and strangers here, looking for the city that hath foundations, whose builder and maker is God.
6. Instead of sorrow's being an evidence of God's wrath, he, in his infinite wisdom and love, is using it as a means of discipline and development that shall better fit us for the joys of heaven. In fact, we have his promise that all things shall work together for our good if we love him. Even Jesus was made perfect through suffering before he could be the Captain of our salvation, and shall we complain if we are required to follow our Leader to perfection and joy, over the same way he walked?

7. The whole life and death of Christ are an evidence, a demonstration, of the possibility that human weakness may so grasp the divine power by faith as to live in this world a righteous life and die a triumphant death.

All these lessons a lost world must learn before it can be redeemed. Jesus taught them all, and he is the Redeemer. In his life and death the whole problem of pain is considered and every question answered, and answered in harmony with a God that is love.

This had been the problem of problems. Every philosophy had dealt with it in vain. Epicureanism,[6] by denying the possibility of a future life, plunged men the more hotly into the mad race for pleasure here, and so multiplied their misery, and made each sorrow an unmixed evil that hid from men the face of a living Father. Stoicism sought to benumb the feelings of man to suffering, and so, in fact, it made them indifferent to the sorrows of others. Buddha gave up the problem. He said that to exist is to suffer, the only rest is in Nirvana. Even Job's comforters answered all these questions wrong; and Job's wife besought him, on account of his sorrow, to curse God and die.

This had been the way of the world,—all men through suffering coming to hate God, and so going constantly into more sin and more suffering, till all knowledge of a God that is love was lost. But after men by wisdom knew not God, it pleased God, through Jesus, to reveal himself and solve all these problems. The only reason that Job did not go with the multitude into cursing and death was that by faith he had grasped the promise and fact of a given Saviour, and through him, of a future where he should "see God," and come to understand all his providences here. And what remains for us? What but patiently, yes, joyfully, to bear all the sorrow that comes, and so fill up that which is behind the sufferings of Christ for his body's sake, which is the church? Why should we not rejoice in tribulation? If we are in prison, Love holds the keys, and we, like Paul, are not prisoners of Caesar, but prisoners of the Lord. Our own good and the good of his cause are one, and when it is for that good, he will release us, as he did Peter.

No sorrow can reach us till his love has transformed it into a blessing. We are made thereby more tender, more kind, our sympathies are broadened, our hearts enlarged, and we are lifted more and more into the atmosphere of divine love, till the atonement is complete, and we become one with suffering humanity, and at the same time one with the Father and one with the Son.

Notes:

1. To deceive; to raise trivial and frivolous objection.
2. Rom. 3:31.
3. The idea of this illustration is borrowed from Walker's "Plan of Salvation."
4. Rom. 3:26.
5. Acts 5:31.
6. The philosophy of Epicurus who subscribed to a hedonistic ethics that considered an imperturbable emotional calm the highest good and whose followers held intellectual pleasures superior to transient sensualism.

XVII

God's Dealing With the Wicked

"He that believeth on the Son hath everlasting life."—John 3:36

"The soul that sinneth, it shall die."—Eze. 18:20

"There shall be no more death."—Rev. 21:4

Having considered the love of God as revealed in his work, as revealed in his law, and as revealed in the atonement by which men are rescued from the ultimate results of the violation of that law, we will now consider that love as revealed in God's dealings with those who persist in sin.

We have seen that all misery is the result of sin, and sin is the violation of God's law. God's law, therefore, is simply the way of happiness and joy. It is the way the redeemed walk when they return and come to Zion, with songs and everlasting joy upon their heads. It may be asked, If God is love, why does sin exist? why was it permitted to exist at all? why is it permitted to continue to exist through these long, weary centuries? and when, and how, if ever, will it be brought to a final end, and the eternal and universal reign of righteousness and peace be ushered in?

We believe these questions can all be reasonably, logically, and consistently answered, and answered in harmony with the character of a God who is love, and only love. Full well we know that the theology of the day cannot deal with these questions satisfactorily, but we believe the theology of the Bible can.

In order that man might be other than a mere automaton, a machine to manifest the mind of God,—in order that he might be a separate personality, capable of living, thinking, and acting for himself, and so capable of honoring God, by returning him love for love, and praise for his goodness,—in order that man might be all this, it was necessary that he be made free. But to make man free was to run the risk of sin. In other words, in order that man might be made capable of being righteous, it was necessary that he be made capable of being wicked. God did not make man wicked; neither did he in the fullest sense make man righteous. He simply made him capable of both; capable of the one, that he might be of the other. God cannot arbitrarily give character, either good or bad; if he could, he would be to blame for not giving all men righteousness, and consequent joy.

There is a difference between innocence and character, either good or bad. Innocence is, in some sense, the absence of character. If I have a blank book, with every page white and clean, unless the language is made to refer exclusively to the mechanical execution of the book, it cannot be said to be either good or bad; it is innocent. As I write in it day by day, it assumes character, and becomes good or bad, according as I write in it good or bad things.

So God made man innocent, and pure, and free to choose, and placed him under conditions favorable to the attainment of a righteous character. He made all intelligent, morally accountable beings in his universe thus. Some of them chose the evil instead of the good, and this accounts for the existence of sin and misery. God did not make sin or misery. It was not an absolute necessity that there should be sin and misery; but it was an absolute necessity that man should be made capable of these, else he could not be capable of righteousness and joy.

No one can deny that God ran the risk of sin, for that would be to deny the existence of sin. This is why he ran that risk, because such risk was necessary to the possibility of righteousness and joy. But eternal sin would be an eternal thwarting of God's plans for a universe where every creature should be rejoicing in his love and returning him praise and thanksgiving. So while God ran the risk of sin, he did not run the risk of eternal sin.

To avoid eternal sin man was given conditional existence and access to the tree of life to perpetuate that existence; but when he had sinned, lest he put forth his hand and take and eat of the tree of life, and live forever, an immortal sinner, the Lord drove him from the garden, and set an angel to guard the way of the tree of life.

Look upon the world as it is, filled with sorrow and suffering. Every city and town has its encampment of "low green tents" where the silent majority are. Every mound holds some heart's treasure. Every hearth has its vacant chair, every heart its haunted chamber where the silent moonlight of regretful memory falls. Each soul knows its own bitterness, and vainly fancies that others walk in the sunlight, while its path only lies in the shadows.

Could the curtain be lifted, and we all see men heart to heart, as now eye to eye, what ghastly revelations of unknown misery would there be! How many a smiling face but seeks, by multiplying the smiles, to hide the heart that is bleeding! If all the misery and suffering of only one city were laid open before our eyes, we should stand aghast with horror; and yet the world is made up of such cities. Ask yourself, would God be good, would he be love, to stamp all this with immortality? The answer is, No! emphatically no! Would he have been either good or wise to have taken any risks of such eternal existence of suffering? Again the answer is, No. But God is good; he is love. Therefore he took no such risks; but he so conditioned immortality on obedience to his divine law as to make sin and misery, if they came, but the children of a few brief years, while righteousness and joy are eternal.

Sin is the cause of all misery. Eternal sin would be eternal misery. Eternal, hopeless sin would be eternal, hopeless misery. The eternal existence of the sinner would be his eternal conscious suffering. The only escape from this is in the assumption of universalism, but this is not only an assumption, but it is in direct contradiction not only to the Bible, but also to all we know of the nature of sin.

We know that the nature of sin is to harden the heart against good influences. The longer it is persisted in, the more sure it is to be continued. It requires no inspired word to reveal to the philosophical mind the fact that to every persistent sinner there comes an end of probation,—a time when sin has so hardened his heart against the influences of good, and so strengthened the influences of evil in their hold upon his nature, that it is an absolute certainty that he will never turn from sin to righteousness. The eternal conscious existence of such an one would be eternal, conscious, hopeless misery, going constantly down into the deeper depths of darkness and despair.

Would God be good to continue such existence forever? Even in the condition of mixed good and evil here, what thoughtful man would choose an eternity of this, if he could? There is truth in the old legend of the life apple, so beautifully wrought into poetic verse by Owen Meredith (Lord Lytton).

An apple was brought to King Solomon from the tree of life, which, if he should but eat of, he would live forever. He philosophizes on life and its failure to satisfy him, and concludes that he does not wish to eat it; but he thinks he knows one of his favorite, light-hearted wives or concubines to whom it will be a great boon. Surely, to her life is all joy, and she will wish it perpetuated. He gives it to her; but she philosophizes also, giving her reasons for not wishing to eat it. She takes it to another; so it passes all ranks of society, from the highest to the lowest, and finally comes back to the king, and is preserved in a silver urn, for no one will eat it.

Even here, so great is the misery that sin has caused, that every thoughtful mind would hesitate to decide that an eternity of this sort of existence was a blessing rather than a curse. But here there remains the hope of something better to come. If all other hopes are gone, to the most despairing soul, who knows nothing of the consolation of God's love, there remains the hope of death,—the thought that the "fitful fever" will soon be over, it will not be long. Take even this hope away, and leave the soul absolutely and hopelessly in immortal despair, to say nothing of any literal fire,—could a God who is love give such an existence to a single creature he has made? The answer must be, No.

Suppose he should put the sinner over into the next world, restored to its Edenic beauty, or over into heaven itself. Sin has brought all the misery into this world; and it would soon make another world as miserable as this. Suppose the sinful souls should be separated, and only a few sinners put in a world where all were righteous. This would be the worst punishment of all. The sinner carries a hell with him, in his own heart, and its fires would burn the hotter in the pure air of heaven. Fancy a man with a burning appetite for drink upon him, walking the golden streets of the New Jerusalem, looking for some place to satisfy his thirst, and finding it not; or a woman whose chief enjoyment here had been to gossip about her neighbors' faults, finding that amusement deprived her there, for the want of material for gossip. Such people would want to emigrate. Suppose you put them where all are wicked and only wicked; there misery would reign supreme.

Now we have seen that God cannot arbitrarily make the sinful soul righteous, for righteousness implies freedom of choice and voluntary action. We have seen, also, that the persistent sinner will not submit to God, to be made righteous of his own free will, for sin constantly hardens his heart more and more. We have seen that an eternity of this sort of life would be a curse and not a blessing; that in a state where all but him were good, he would be utterly miserable; and that if put where all were bad, misery would there reign supreme.

What is the one thing that infinite, omnipotent Love can do with such a one, and still be true to himself?—He can take away the existence he has given him, because he has failed to meet the object of that existence, to fill the place for which he was created. This is justice, this is love, and this God will do; for he says, "Yet a little while, and the wicked shall not be; yea, thou shalt diligently consider his place, and it shall not be."[1] "They shall be as though they had not been."[2]

This is not only the best, the most loving thing that can be done to the sinner himself, but, when we consider the interests of the righteous, its love is more manifest. From the very nature of sin, and of man as a social being, we have seen that we must bear the consequences of one another's sorrows and sins. This must continue as long as sin continues. But Jesus suffered, the just for the unjust, *that he might bring us, the unjust ones, to God.* We will not complain, but rather rejoice to take part in that suffering, for that purpose; but when the time comes that the last persistent sinner is so hardened that he will not be touched by this suffering love and brought back to God, why should we suffer longer? That were hopeless, useless suffering. God is love, and he will not permit his children thus to suffer.

Jesus permits us to suffer here with him, as he suffered, and for the same purpose, that we too might be made perfect through suffering, while bringing others to him; but when we have been perfected, and all others that can be brought to him by our suffering love have come to him, so that those who remain are only worthless, hopeless chaff, then "the Son of man shall send forth his angels, and they shall gather out of his kingdom all things that offend, and them which do iniquity. . . . Then shall the righteous shine forth as the sun in the kingdom of their Father." "What is the chaff to the wheat? saith the Lord." "God will gather the wheat into his garner, but the chaff will he burn with unquenchable fire."

Says Paul to the faithful, "All things are yours, . . . whether the world, or life, or death, or things present, or things to come; all are yours, and ye are Christ's; and Christ is God's."

We, with David, have sometimes been tempted to fret because of the apparent prosperity of the wicked here, but all things are ours. The wicked may hold our inheritance for a time, leaving us pilgrims and strangers here. Shall we complain, when Jesus said of himself, "The foxes have holes, and the birds of the air have nests; but the Son of man hath not where to lay his head"?—Ah, no! but rather let us look with joyful anticipation to the time when the kingdoms of this world shall become the kingdoms of our Lord and his Christ; for when they are his, they are ours; for he is ours, and we are his. "And the kingdom and dominion, and the greatness of the kingdom under the whole heaven, shall be given to the people of the saints of the Most High, whose kingdom is an everlasting kingdom, and all dominions shall serve and obey him."

Love has had this in view from the beginning, when he made the world for his glory and pleasure and for the joy of his children. In spite of sin and sorrow, Love has ever been reaching forth toward this grand realization, and the kingdom will come. Jesus taught his disciples to pray that prayer, "Our Father who art in heaven, hallowed be thy name. Thy kingdom come." That prayer has been prayed devoutly and earnestly by the waiting, weeping church through all these centuries. It has gone up from dungeons, from mountain caves, and from the martyr's funeral pyre of flame. And it will be answered. Love in patience waits, not willing that any should perish, but that all should come to repentance. "As I live, saith the Lord God, I have no pleasure in the death of the wicked; but that the wicked turn from his way and live; turn ye, turn ye from your evil ways; for why will ye die?"

Yet the chaff must be destroyed and the kingdom returned to the faithful. This is why God destroys the wicked. He is love, and it is best for all that the wicked should be destroyed. Then the kingdom shall be restored to the righteous, and "every creature which is in heaven, and on the earth, and under the earth, and such as are in the sea, and all that are in them," will be heard saying, "Blessing, and honor, and glory, and power, be unto him that sitteth upon the throne, and unto the Lamb forever and ever." Love's object will be accomplished at last, and its constant manifestation will bring universal acknowledgment, and unbroken, unbounded return of love.

Notes:

1. Ps. 37:10.
2. Obadiah 10.

XVIII

Why Has Sin Been Permitted So Long?

"Love suffereth long, and is kind."—1 Cor. 13:13

"The Lord is . . . longsuffering to us-ward, not willing that any should perish."—2 Peter 3:9

The existence of sin and its resulting misery do not in the least antagonize the idea that God is love, and only love. The possibility of sin was a necessity to love's realization. Every parent who brings a child into the world to satisfy the God-implanted paternal instinct of love, runs the same risk. The child may be a blessing or he may be a curse to his kind; nevertheless, the risk must be run, or the very existence of the race must discontinue, and not only God's love but all fatherly love be defrauded of its realization.

We have seen how God is to bring sin to an end, so that every creature in heaven and in earth will finally be found pouring forth its thankful praise for an existence which, being perfect joy, will be love's highest possible realization. This will be accomplished by so manifesting his love as to win all that can be won to holiness and happiness. The redeemed world will then be peopled with these, and all others will be as though they had not been. This is the best that infinite Love can do for all his creatures, best for both the saved and the lost.

However, the question still remains, Why has sin been permitted to continue so long? Why have the weary centuries dragged by so slowly, laden with their weight of woe? Why has not Love brought the final triumph ere this, and the release of his children from misery and pain? Certainly God knew who would be incorrigibly sinful; why did he not destroy Satan and his angels in the very beginning, nor suffer them to tempt the human race? Why, when Adam and Eve sinned, did he not destroy them, and create other two to people this world, nor suffer the curse of sin to continue thus till the world itself was ruined, and every hill and vale was stained with blood and bedewed with tears?

It must be remembered that the conflict between good and evil is not confined to this world. It is a universal conflict. And why?—Simply because, as God made man free, and thereby ran the risk of sin, for that same reason he made the angels free, he made all his morally accountable beings to people all worlds, free. In fact, they could not have been morally accountable had they not been free. Thus the risk of sin was a universal risk. I do not say that sin itself was universal; I do not believe this; but the conflict between sin and righteousness is universal.

Part of the angels sinned, and they have, with their prince, Satan himself, been mustering and leading the forces of evil ever since. Part of the angels did not sin, and they, with Prince Emanuel, the Captain of our salvation, have been leading the forces of righteousness ever since. The battle we are fighting here is the same that began up in heaven, when Michael fought, and Satan fought, and their angels. There is not one intelligent, morally responsible being of all the untold millions that people the uncounted worlds but is interested in this conflict, and, in some sense, at least, has part in it. All were made free and placed upon probation, as were men and angels. Sometime the conflict will be over, and the victory won for truth and right; then the probation of all will close, and all the victors will be confirmed in their immortality.

We know not how many of these worlds have been untouched by sin. It may be that the fallen angels and man are the only ones at war with God. This we do know, our God is the God of hosts. When the conflict goes hard around us, and we see sin on every hand, we sometimes think that the truly righteous are diminished from the earth, and, with Elijah, almost fear that we are alone, and that all others have bowed the knee to Baal. At such times we need only to look up with the eye of faith to know that we are a part of the mighty majority, and that our Commander, at the head of his hosts, leads to victory.

But what has all this to do with the continuance of sin? We answer,

Much; everything, in fact. God does nothing arbitrarily. He made us all free to choose between good and evil. He will never violate that freedom in one of his creatures. The whole conflict between truth and error, between right and wrong, must be fought out to the final conclusion before the eyes of all. That conclusion depends upon the power of truth and right to conquer finally on a fair field, in the minds of free, intelligent beings.

God is on trial. Satan has accused him of being hard and unjust; he has said that his laws are arbitrary and severe. To the universe of intelligent beings God says, "Ye are my witnesses, saith the Lord, that I am God,"—that is, that I am good, that my laws and dealings with my creatures are love's own; in short, that God is love.

But all this takes some time. Suppose God had blotted Satan and his angels out of existence when they first sinned. His only object in doing this would have been to put an end to sin and misery right there. Would it have accomplished that object?

Satan was an honored angel in heaven, one of the leaders of the heavenly hosts. They had not seen the terrible nature of sin. In fact they had not really seen Satan do any great evil. He had simply accused God, and said he was arbitrary and hard. This very accusation put God on trial before the free minds of his creatures. Was it true or false? If God had then and there blotted out the hosts of evil, before evil was allowed to develop and reveal its true nature, would not those who remained have said that the accusations of Satan were just, and that God had in that very act proved himself guilty? But this would be, not to put an end to sin, but rather to perpetuate and multiply it. The very object of God in doing that would thus have been defeated. God was too wise for that.

When the soldiers enlisted in our great rebellion, they enlisted, not to free the slaves, that was not yet the issue of the war, but to put down the rebellion. There was a class of men, sneeringly called Abolitionists, who believed the slaves should be freed. They sent a delegation down to President Lincoln, beseeching him to make that the issue of the war. They brought argument after argument, but the president was unmoved. They went away, perhaps thinking that the heart of Lincoln was not in sympathy with their desires. Such, however, was not the case. Lincoln loved and pitied the poor slaves; he had not only love but wisdom. He knew that to make emancipation the issue of the war then, would to a large extent disband the Northern army, and so defeat that very issue. It is a fact that, even when emancipation was proclaimed, one regiment of Northern soldiers stacked their arms, and said that they did not enlist to fight to free the negroes. Even they, however, afterward resumed their arms, and fought with the bravest and best. Why?—Slavery had been allowed to develop itself until it was seen that it meant the destruction of the Union. The Union could not be preserved, guaranteeing our national greatness, without freeing the slaves. It was this conviction, and this only, which rested in the minds of the Northern soldiers, and made them stand by Lincoln in that emancipation proclamation, and fight till the slaves were free.

So sin must be allowed to develop until all God's free, intelligent creatures shall see that sin is misery and that righteousness is joy; and this is the very reason why God in love said, "Thou shalt not," and "Thou shalt." There is nothing arbitrary here. God is acquitted. His pleasure and glory are the highest possible joy of all his creatures. Sin, successfully continued and carried out, means the overthrow of God's government, the dethroning of God himself, and the destruction of his pleasure and glory; hence sin is misery, and not joy. Universal and eternal sin would be universal and eternal misery. God is acquitted, and Satan is convicted.

When sin is developed until this is seen, then God can put an end to sin, and destroy the incorrigibly sinful, and every creature in his universe will unite with him in this judgment, and pronounce him just. This is why the righteous participate with him in judgment. It is thus the whole conflict will be brought to an end, and the victory be final, so that "affliction shall not rise up a second time."

All this will be done, and yet the perfect freedom of every individual mind be maintained through it all. And when the finally redeemed pour forth their unceasing and universal song of praise and adoration, that song will come from souls who are free from sin, and yet who retain the full power to sin,—separate, conscious, intelligent entities, who will never sin, simply because they have learned to love righteousness and hate evil. They will thus be beings capable of appreciating a God who is love, and so capable of giving him return of love. This was God's object in creating the worlds, and Satan and sin will not defeat it, nor rob him of his longed-for love.

When the trial and the conflict are ended, the final verdict, poured forth in wondering praise from the still *free* minds and hearts of all intelligent beings, will be, "Great and marvelous are thy works, Lord God Almighty; *just and true* are thy ways, thou King of saints." Worthy is the Lord that created, worthy is the Lamb that was slain, to receive power, and riches, and wisdom, and strength, and honor, and glory, and blessings.

Satan will not only find himself unable to defeat the plan of God, but he will not even defer it for a year or a day. When man sinned, God said to him, in substance, "I will greatly multiply thy seed."[1] Why did he do this? If man had not sinned, at some definite time known to God, the world would have been peopled with righteous beings, who had passed their probationary period, and been confirmed in their immortality. When man sinned, he greatly multiplied the seed, that out of the multitudes that should be born and die, he, through Christ, could in this same time gather this same number that should "be accounted to him for a generation."

He knoweth the day and the hour, and when the dispensation of the fullness of time is come, all things will have been gathered in Christ, and God's original plan and purpose will be complete. The universe will know then that, if Satan is "mighty," God is almighty, and that therefore no power can delay his plans.

Our little lives are lived down here in the valley of trial and darkness, and the time to us seems long; but what are six thousand years compared to eternity? Says the Lord: "For a *small moment* have I forsaken thee,"—apparently, as compared with the future redeemed state,—"for a small moment have I forsaken thee; but with great mercies will I gather thee. In a little wrath I hid my face from thee for a moment; but with everlasting kindness will I have mercy on thee, saith the Lord thy Redeemer."[2]

When a few million years have been spent in the full joy of the redeemed, former things will not be remembered nor come into mind. Not that there will be any arbitrary loss of memory, for that would involve the loss of identity; but no shade of past sadness will rest for a moment on the soul. The redeemed who have lived long on the height of Beulah, if they cast a backward glance, will look from hilltop to hilltop, from the paradise that has been gained to the paradise that was lost. If the valley of sin and suffering, the small moment of his wrath, be thought of at all, it will be only that our present joy may be increased thereby, and our love to him be magnified by the marvelous revelation, through redemption, of the great fact that God is love.

Notes:

1. Gen. 3:10.
2. Isa. 54:7, 8.

XIX

Will There Be Gain?

"Ours the seed-time, God alone
Beholds the end of what is sown;
Beyond our vision, weak and dim.
The harvest time is hid with him."

—Whittier

We have seen why sin exists, and why it has been permitted to exist so long. Through the mystery of God, the mystery of iniquity is explained. The Lion of the tribe of Judah is found worthy to open the book and to unloose the seals thereof. We have seen also how sin will be brought to an end, and the glory of God revealed, so that all flesh shall see it together. One question more remains on this point: Will there be any gain to God and to his creatures as the result of sin and redemption? When redemption is complete, will the world and the universe be just where it would have been had sin never existed? or will there be a more perfect safety against sin in the future, a higher, and deeper, and broader knowledge of God's love, and so a grander joy and greater peace than would otherwise have been possible?[1]

We see a law of suffering running through this world. That suffering is not useless; it is permitted for the good of others. The flower dies that the fruit may have birth. The storm that destroys one man's life and property, banishes malaria, destroys the dangerous germs, and fills the air with new life-giving power, thus blessing thousands, so that through the loss of some life and joy much life and joy have been gained.

Almost every truth that blesses the world has had its martyrs. The few have suffered and died; the many have gained new life and joy thereby. In order that the new tree may grow and bless the earth with its beauty and shade and luscious fruit, the seed must die. On every hand the mystery of this death out of which life springs is manifest. Is this a law of this world simply? or is it in some sense universal? Does it apply only to certain isolated cases of suffering and death? or does it include all suffering and all death? Is God's plan so perfect and so broad as to leave no possible room for real loss, but to make everything minister to greater gain?

We have seen that Satan will not be able to defeat, or even to defer, the full realization of God's plan and purpose. Dare we ask the question, Is it possible that he is only a part of that plan?—not that God ever wished Satan or any one else to sin, far less that he ever forced him to it.

God made the inhabitants of all worlds free, and works with them only through the medium of their free wills. But by making them free he ran the risk of sin. This was done in all the countless millions of worlds made and peopled by him. A continued risk implies a final certainty. Was it God's purpose, when sin came, so to use it as to make it minister to a higher holiness and a greater possible joy for all his creatures? Can it be that the sum total of all joy is to be increased rather than diminished by the sum total of all suffering? This would be like an omnipotent, omniscient God,—a God who says he is love. Is it possible that God's plan is so broad as to include all other plans, so that even Satan, with all his rebellious schemes, falls in as a part of the great harmonious whole that lifts the universe into a full realization of love's ideal? Fortunately, we are not left to speculate on this question. Paul says, "All things work together for good to them that love God." In this very connection he is speaking of tribulation, and persecution, and famine, and nakedness, and peril, and sword,—in short, of suffering and all the results of sin.

He does not say all these things are good. They are the results of sin, and sin is bad, and so these are bad. God hates them more than we can, because he loves all his creatures more than we do. When God's ideal is realized, there will be no place in his universe for one throb of pain or one moan of anguish. All this will be past then, for it is bad. But what the text says is that all this works together for good to them that love God. Notice how broad this statement is,—"all things." That includes all suffering as well as all joy. It includes every result of sin. "To them that love God" includes not only every righteous son and daughter of Adam, but every righteous, intelligent being, every one of all the hosts that shall people the universe when redemption is complete.

It is evident that if this is true in the life of every righteous individual, it is true in the sum total of all righteous lives. If each and every experience of suffering works together for good in the life of each and every one who loves God, then all suffering works together for the good of all who love God. But all suffering is the result of sin, therefore, in some way, God is to make the very existence of sin minister to the higher good of all who love him, that is, of all who shall people his universe after redemption is complete.

In this life of trial and suffering the highest possible joy that Christianity can bring to the individual comes in the firm faith in this fact; so the highest possible conception and the greatest possible consciousness of God's love will come to the universe in the broader belief in this fact for all.

Some may say, How can these things be? Whether we understand them or not, we must believe them if we believe God's word. This we do know, that perfect joy can come only through perfection of character, and in some sense even Jesus was made perfect through suffering. All his suffering was the result of sin, though not of his own sin. Even Jesus will be raised to a higher joy and a greater honor than would have been possible for him had it not been for sin. Through his suffering and humiliation to redeem the world, he will be highly exalted, and given a name that is above every name, "that at the name of Jesus every knee should bow, of things in heaven, and things in earth, and things under the earth; and that every tongue should confess that Jesus Christ is Lord, to the glory of God the Father." Isaiah says, "He shall see of the travail of his soul, and shall be satisfied." This will be true not only of Christ, but of all Christians. With David we shall be satisfied when we awake in his likeness. We shall see that the sorrow and suffering we have passed through here have made us capable of a higher joy throughout eternity.

It has been said that our knowledge consists solely in a recognition of likeness and difference. This is certain. If all things tasted the same, the very ideas of sweet and sour would not exist; if all things looked the same tint, the idea of color would be impossible. If some one came from some other world where there was flavor and color, and told us of these things, we could even then have only a vague idea of them. So man through sin came not only to know evil, but to know "both good and evil." The inhabitants of other worlds may know much more of us than we do of them. Angels are their tutors as they were ours before the fall, and they may even have the privilege and power of visiting this world with the angels. Certain it is, the whole record of sin and of redemption from sin will be open for their inspection.

All the misery that has resulted from sin is a revelation of that wisdom and love that said, "Thou shalt not." It is through the mighty contrast of sin and righteousness,—the mystery of iniquity, which is the mystery of self-exaltation, leading down into an infinite degradation; and the mystery of God, which is the mystery of divine humiliation, exalting man to an equality with the angels, and lifting even Christ himself to higher honor and joy,—it is through this mighty contrast spread out before the universe that all intelligent beings will come so to know good and evil, so to love righteousness and hate iniquity, that the danger of sin will be overpast.

What could God's creatures have known of his love if it had not been for sin and redemption? They could see his love as revealed in his work, but what is this to the higher love revealed through redemption? This is a love into which the angels desire to look,—a love which even they fail to fathom. If even now we could leave this world of sin and suffering, and, of the angels that before the throne bathe ever in the perfect light of love divine, ask what most they thought revealed the love of God, they would answer, "God so loved the world, that he gave his only begotten Son." Even they, with all God's creatures, will know more of his love than they could have known if it had not been for sin and redemption from sin; and knowing more of that love, they will rest safer and surer in that love, and so know a deeper joy.

Grace is unmerited favor. What could God's children have known of his grace if all had ever merited his favor? Mercy is another attribute of God. He says his mercy is from everlasting to everlasting. Mercy is the disposition to treat an offender better than he deserves. Suppose there had never been an offender in God's universe; what could his children have known of his infinite mercy? The whole plan of redemption is the most marvelous manifestation conceivable of his grace and mercy. But grace and mercy are only different names for, or, rather, different manifestations of, love. So this is only another way of showing that through sin and redemption God will make a fuller revelation of his love than would have been possible if sin had not existed.

But to see God as thus revealed, to know him, is everlasting life; and everlasting life is everlasting joy. It is thus that the little pain of the few, for this brief "moment," will work out the greater joy of the many throughout eternity. What wonder that Paul said, "Our light affliction, which is but for a moment, worketh for us a far more exceeding and eternal weight of glory"!

The fourth and fifth chapters of Revelation each closes with a grand doxology of praise. That of the fourth chapter is based wholly upon creation, that of the fifth, on redemption. Compare the two. The fourth chapter says:—

> "Thou art worthy, O Lord, to receive glory and honor and power; for thou hast created all things, and for thy pleasure they are and were created."

The fifth chapter says:—

> "Worthy is the Lamb that was slain to receive power, and riches, and wisdom, and strength, and honor, and glory, and blessing. And every creature which is in heaven, and on the earth, and under the earth, and such as are in the sea, and all that are in them, heard I saying, Blessing, and honor, and glory, and power, be unto him that sitteth upon the throne, and unto the Lamb forever and ever."

The excess of praise and joyful adoration in the last over the first is the gain to God and his creatures through sin and redemption. Paul says he preached the unsearchable riches of Christ "to make all men see what is the fellowship of the mystery, which from the beginning of the world hath been hid in God, who created all things by Jesus Christ; to the intent that now unto the principalities and powers in heavenly places might be known by the church the manifold wisdom of God." And the wisdom of God is the wisdom of that love which said, "Thou shalt not" and "Thou shalt." Other translations give, instead of "heavenly places," *heavenlies,* or *heavenly worlds.*

Who has the grandest character here? he who has been nursed in ease and luxury, knowing nothing of trial, or he who has come up through hardship and struggle, and conquered them all? Which will make the best teacher? Why should not the church of Christ, those who have come up through great tribulation, and who have conquered in his might,—why should not they be used by him to initiate the inhabitants of other worlds, untouched by sin, into the deeper mysteries of his love and holiness? And so they will, for it is said they shall be kings and priests unto God, and Paul immediately goes on to speak of that love which passes knowledge, and of the fact that unto God will be glory *in the church* by Christ Jesus, throughout all ages, world without end.

It is thus seen that Satan is outwitted and outgeneraled by God at every point. All his planning and scheming for defeating God's purpose of love have been only a part of God's larger plan by which love's ideal will be realized. The death of Jesus was the work of the devil, the greatest manifestation of sin. Satan thought thereby to thwart the plan and purpose of God, but Paul says of that very death that Jesus triumphed over principalities and powers, in it making a show of them openly. These were the principalities and powers of evil, with Satan at their head. Thus what Satan fancied was his greatest victory was really God's greatest victory over him,—a victory which will finally destroy him and his, and unite the universe under the mild and loving sway of Prince Emanuel. It is thus that God maketh the wrath of man, and of devils too, to praise him, and the remainder of wrath—all that he cannot make work for good,—will he restrain.

It is ever thus in our lives. The hour of the greatest temptation and darkness may be, through him, the hour of the greatest triumph. From the very valley of the shadow of death we may rise to a new life and a new joy, for all things work together for good to them that love God, and to love God is to know that God is love.

Notes:

1. When we speak of a certain thing as being possible and another thing as being impossible with God, we wish to be understood to mean that it is impossible with him only in so far as our human comprehension of him is concerned,—that is, it is unthinkable to the human mind that it should be possible. In one sense, with God nothing is impossible, but in another sense this is not true, for God works through means, that is, through his laws, and he has chosen to limit himself by these laws. He wills all men to be saved, but he has so constructed the universe that the free choice of good is necessary to salvation; he therefore cannot compel men to be good. He cannot save men against their wills, nor can he arbitrarily control their wills. We do not absolutely know that he could not have made the universe in some other way, but to us this is unthinkable; besides, if he could, and thus have avoided the risk of sin, and still reached the end of universal righteousness and joy, why did he not do it that way? The inference is that the way he did it is the best and only good way. The same is true of his taking advantage of sin to reveal his love and mercy and grace, so as to lift men into higher possible joy. It is unthinkable to the human mind that the same knowledge of God and the same joy could be reached any other way. If they could, why did not God do it that way, and so reach this end without sin or the danger of sin's entering his universe? God never either forced or beguiled any one into sin, but he is omniscient. He knew that some would sin, and laid his plan accordingly, taking advantage of sin to reveal his greatest love, and so to lead his creatures to the highest joy. It is reasonable to believe that when the end is reached, the redeemed will see that it has been reached in the best way.

XX

The Closing of Probation

"The Lord is good; his mercy is everlasting, and his truth endureth to all generations."

—Ps. 100:5

We often hear the expression, "while mercy lasts," or, "till mercy ends." These expressions are not only unscriptural in themselves, but the idea they carry with them is foreign to the whole Bible, and entirely contrary to the character of God. The thought that oftentimes underlies them is something like this: God is merciful now, but the time is coming when he will cease to be merciful. God accepts repentance now, but the time is coming when men may repent ever so sincerely, but it will be too late, God will not accept that repentance. God loves the sinner now, but the time is coming when that love will turn into consuming anger and unrestrained wrath.

Nothing could be more absolutely false than such ideas. But says one, Do you not believe, does not the Bible plainly teach, that there is to be such a thing as the closing of probation? We answer, Most certainly. And will not sinful man sustain a different relation to God then than now? If he is not saved before that time, will not his salvation then be impossible? Again we answer, Yes, to both of these questions. Where, then, is the fallacy in these expressions? It is in the idea running through them all that God changes, and that it is to be some change in his feelings toward sinful man that is to bring about the close of probation.

A change there is to be, bringing that awful hour when the destiny of all men will be unalterably fixed, when he that is righteous will be righteous still, and he that is filthy will be filthy still; but that change is wholly in man, not in God.

The very word "God" means good. The psalmist says, "From everlasting to everlasting, thou art God." That is, from everlasting to everlasting thou art the supreme, the over-ruling, the all-embracing and all-unchanging Good. Says the Lord: "I change not;" "with me there is no variableness, neither shadow of turning." "Jesus Christ is the same yesterday, today, and forever." He is himself the "Everlasting Father" of all created beings; he inhabiteth eternity. Knowing all the future, with its terrible climax of guilt and rebellion, as well as all the past, with its history of repeated and constant wanderings from him, he is not disturbed or surprised into anger by any sudden development of sin. Wonderful as it may seem, with the whole dark fact of sin, past and future, spread out before him, he still loves us with an "everlasting love," and with loving-kindness he has ever sought to draw us to him. David says, "The Lord is good; his mercy is everlasting, and his truth endureth to all generations."

All this is sufficient to show that whatever change there is in bringing about the close of probation, that change is not in God, but in man. "I have not forsaken you, saith the Lord, but ye have forsaken me."

God is love; he is everlasting love. He never has and never will forsake any one; but men forsake him, the Fountain of living water, and then hew out for themselves cisterns, broken cisterns, that can hold no water. The world will finally forsake God entirely, and give themselves over wholly to the last great delusion of error. This is the closing of probation. The study of the closing of probation is the study of the unpardonable sin.

Jesus Christ, in infinite love, and by the power of the Spirit of God, was healing diseases, forgiving sins, and casting out devils. There were those who, looking on, admitted that never man spake such words or wrought such works; and yet they were so blinded and hardened by sin that they failed to distinguish between the supreme Spirit of good and the supreme spirit of evil. They said, "He casts out devils by Beelzebub, the prince of devils." Jesus said this sin could not be forgiven them, neither in this world nor in the world to come. Why was this? Was it because the sin was so great that it made the Lord so angry he could never get over it? This would be to make God altogether such an one as ourselves, only greater, and more furious, and more enduring in his wrath. He requires us to forgive the repentant one without limit, and will he not do the same? He condemns the holding of anger in us, and does he hold hatred himself? This would be his requiring us to be holy as he is not. Says Whittier:—

"The wrong that pains my soul below
I dare not throne above."

There must be some other reason why that sin is unpardonable. God made men free to choose between the right and the wrong. If they had chosen the right and continued in that way, by the very law of heredity and the law of the influence of environment the power of the good over them would soon have become so strengthened, and the power of the evil so weakened, that the danger of sinning would be overpast. But men chose the evil and continued in it, thus turning those beneficent laws against themselves. Through the working of those same laws, the power of good over us has become so weakened, and the power of sin so strengthened, that men are born slaves to sin.

God gives us his Spirit to restore this freedom that has been lost through sin. It was because the Spirit of the Lord was upon Jesus that he came to proclaim liberty to the captive. Jesus said, "No man can come to me, except the Father which hath sent me draw him;" and again, "No man can come unto me except it were given unto him of my Father." Not that God draws some and does not draw others, and so makes salvation possible only to the favored few; for the same Jesus says, "I, if I be lifted up from the earth, will draw all men unto me,"—not compel them to come, but draw them, so as to make it possible for them to come,—so as to restore the freedom that has been lost through sin.

The Spirit of God would never have striven with men if it had not been for the plan of redemption, which centers in Christ; but now through him all men are set free. He is the Light that lighteth every man that cometh into the world. That Spirit reaches us just where we are, taking all the circumstances of birth, of heredity, and of environment into consideration. By it the balance of the mind is restored, so that "whosoever will may come." This gives man a second chance; but if man resists the Spirit, and chooses the evil again, he again makes himself a slave. Sin, persisted in, hardens the heart against the influence of the Spirit of God, and strengthens the power of evil over us, until a point is reached where it is absolutely certain that we will never turn and repent. Whenever any man has become so hardened and blinded by sin as to be unable to distinguish between the workings of the Spirit of God and the workings of Satan, that point has been reached by him, and that man's probation is at an end. This is why the sin against the Holy Spirit is unpardonable.

God can never pardon any sin till it is repented of. It is the goodness of God manifested through his Spirit that leads us to repentance. But how can that Spirit lead a man to repentance toward God when he attributes the very working of that Spirit upon his own heart to the devil and not to God? Manifestly it cannot. That man's probation is closed. God is just the same; his mercy and love and tender pity have not changed; but the man, by persisting in sin, has cut himself off from God, and put himself outside of the plan of redemption. The sin is unpardonable because it is unrepentable.

This is the terrible danger of sin. Every ray of light resisted, every willful sin committed, brings the man nearer that point where the current is so strong and the strength so slight that there is no returning. We cannot tell, but God knows, when any man reaches this point; and when he does, his probation is ended.

Now what is the closing of probation for the world? This is certain, it is not the limit of God's love for the world. God has a great truth for the inhabitants of earth. The everlasting gospel in its fullness is to be preached to every nation, kindred, tongue, and people. The message is a marking one; it marks those who obey, or seals them for God; it marks those who disobey, or seals them for the "beast." (Read the thirteenth and fourteenth chapters of Revelation.)

What does this mean? Simply this: Some accept the light ray by ray, as God gives it. Step by step they are led on till they become sanctified through the truth. Every step makes their hearts tenderer and more susceptible, and places them more completely under the control of the power of God, till finally in their mouth is found no guile, and they follow the Lamb whithersoever he goeth. God's law is imprinted by his Spirit in their hearts, and they are marked before earth and heaven as his. Others reject the light as it comes till the light within them becomes darkness. Their heart becomes harder and harder, and their spiritual eyesight is dimmed.

God is working with mighty power; the message is going with a "loud cry." Satan is also working with all deceivableness of unrighteousness in them that perish.

In each man's life there comes a time when he must make his final choice between right and wrong. If he chooses wrong, he accepts the work of Satan as the great power of God, and rejects the work of God's Spirit as the work of Satan. When he does this finally, he has committed the unrepentable, and therefore the unpardonable sin. He does not do it all at once, but step by step. In resisting the light, his heart is hardened, and he is led up to this final stand; and when this place is reached and this stand taken, the man's probation is at an end. He is marked, or sealed, for the "beast," or Satan.

The message goes on with increasing power. Men continue to resist it. Another takes his final stand, then another, another, and another; the time comes when every man that has not accepted the truth and been sealed for God has finally rejected it, and attributed all its power to Satan. They have all committed the sin that is unpardonable, because it puts the man beyond the reach of the Spirit which leads to repentance. When this point is reached, there is no reason for the work to continue longer. The awful voice of God is heard announcing the solemn fact that all men have made their final choice, and that he that is filthy will be filthy still.

This is not God saying, I have changed, but it is God saying to sinful man, You have changed. It is not God saying, I will not accept repentance and forgive sins any more, but it is God saying, Man will not give repentance and so permit me to forgive sins any more.

If the ministration in the heavenly sanctuary is over and the door of the temple closed, it is not that God is weary of dispensing pardon and mercy, but that there are no more applicants for pardon and mercy. God is the same; his mercy endureth forever; his love is infinite and eternal. When Jesus said to the Jewish people, "O Jerusalem, Jerusalem, which killest the prophets, and stonest them that are sent unto thee; how often would I have gathered thy children together, as a hen doth gather her brood under her wings, and ye would not!" "If thou hadst known, even thou, at least in this thy day, the things which belong unto thy peace! but now they are hid from thine eyes,"—that was the closing of probation to the Jewish people as a nation. The national promises that God had made and conditioned on their obedience were now forever slipping from their grasp. As the destruction of Jerusalem imaged the final destruction, so this imaged the final close of probation.

But these words did not come from an angry, revengeful God; they came from the great heart of tender, pitying, yearning, yet forsaken love. Jesus was weeping. This is God, for God is love. "As I live, saith the Lord God, I have no pleasure in the death of the wicked; but that the wicked turn from his way and live; turn ye, turn ye from your evil ways; for why will ye die?" No man will ever genuinely repent and God not accept him. If he did refuse to accept the repentant sinner, he would deny himself.

Some may think of the passage in Amos where it speaks of the famine for the word of the Lord, and says they shall wander from sea to sea seeking the word of the Lord, and shall not find it. It is true this refers to that time, but who is it that thus seeks the word of the Lord and finds it not? The next verse tells: "They that swear by the sin of Samaria, and say, Thy God, O Dan, liveth." The sin of Samaria was the sin of mingling the worship of God with sun worship. The god of Dan was an Egyptian sun god. This refers to the time when their false theocracy has failed to satisfy and give them the peace that they sought. As the prophet says, instead of realizing their fanatical ideals, "they pass through it, hardly bestead and hungry," and they curse their king and their god (Satan, who is leading them) and look upwards. Why do they not find forgiveness and see the light?—Because they still cling to their sun worship, and swear that it is of the Lord. As Moore says:—

"Faith, fanatic faith, once wedded fast
To some dear falsehood, hugs it to the last."

God cannot accept them, for they will not accept him and his truth. They feel their need of something, but, blinded and hardened by sin, they still attribute the Lord's work to Satan, and are looking for something else, and trying to make the Lord come to their terms.

While these thoughts reveal to us a God whose love is infinite and unchanging throughout eternity, they also reveal the terrible hardening, blinding nature of sin, every step in which brings us nearer the point where return is impossible. In fact, by revealing the terrible nature of sin they reveal the love of that Father that said of sin, "Thou shalt not, my child, thou shalt not."

XXI

"His Strange Act"

"The Lord shall rise up as in Mount Perazim, he shall be wroth as in the valley of Gibeon, that he may do his work, his strange work; and bring to pass his act, his strange act."

—Isa. 28:21

It has been the object of this little book to show that all God's acts in his dealings with humanity come from the motive of love. Against this proposition it is often urged that his vengeful wrath destroyed the old world by a flood, and that a little later that same wrath obliterated entirely the fair cities of the plain, leaving only the dull surges of the Dead Sea to sing their requiem. He also exterminated the Canaanitish tribes, man, woman, and child, and gave their lands and their homes to others.

These things, as recorded in the Bible, it is thought reveal the character of the Jewish Jehovah and the Christian's God as anything but love. We may agree that there are some things here we cannot understand, because we do not know all the circumstances connected with them. I firmly believe, however, that the application to these special cases of the principles already made plain in these chapters will relieve them of very much of their difficulty.

We have seen what the closing of probation is,—that hardening of the heart against the power of truth and righteousness which is the natural result of persistent sinning. There is no limit to God's mercy and love; but as righteousness in the individual soul is the result of God's working in and through that soul, when it is of its own free will submitted to him, the power of God to save men from sin into righteousness is limited by their willingness to submit themselves to him. When that willingness or power is lost through rebellion continued till the habits of the mind have become fixed, then the case is hopeless.

Not certain individuals simply, but the world, is to come to that place at the last, and then the world's probation will be at an end. The world came to that place once before. Every imagination of the heart was only evil, and evil continually. Through continued sinning, generation after generation, the world became so wicked that the nobler desires were either wholly obliterated or hopelessly under the control of the baser passions. Through the laws of heredity and environment this tendency to sin was transmitted to the child even before it was born, and forced upon him by his surroundings from his earliest conscious moment. This had gone so far that even the children were hopelessly enslaved. This also was the condition of the cities of Sodom and Gomorrah, and of the Canaanitish tribes after they had filled up the cup of their iniquity.

We have seen that sin is misery. Continued, hopeless sin is continued, hopeless misery. This is the one thing that Love cannot permit, but the only alternative at such times is destruction. We have seen that it was love that guarded the way of the tree of life, lest men eat and live forever, immortal sinners; and we have seen that it will be Love that destroys the wicked at last. But every reason that love has for the final destruction of the wicked, it also had for the destruction of the old world and the cities of the plain, and for the extermination of the Canaanitish tribes. Indeed, these are all taken by inspiration as images of the future destruction, and are set forth as ensamples to them who should afterward live ungodly. To have continued their existence would have been not only to continue their own misery, but to continue the bringing into existence of millions of children with a heredity and an environment which would make their continued sin and suffering a certainty from the very start.

The existence of such nations or cities in the world is also a constant menace to the happiness and virtue of all others. When a cancerous humor has fastened itself upon the hand, or the gangrene is persistently at work in the foot, it may seem cruel to amputate the member, but at such times Love holds the knife. The difference between murderous savagery and the most heroic love may not be a difference in the act itself, but only a difference in the motive which underlies the act.

This being true, it is not strange that those who have persistently misunderstood God's character in almost everything, should have in this attributed to him the wrong motive. He who knows, both from experience and revelation, that God is love, and who keeps ever before him the fact that love takes no pleasure in death and destruction, will behold, even in these otherwise dark deeds, the revelation of the same watchful, all-embracing, and heroically unselfish Love that withheld not his own and only Son, but freely delivered him up for us all.

God takes no pleasure in the death of the wicked; but that which considers its own pleasure as of the first importance, is not love at all, but selfishness. True love always regards the welfare of the object loved as of first importance, and such love often compels its possessor to do that which grieves him to the heart. It is thus the true father is compelled at times to punish the child; it is thus our Father has dealt with the world, and it is thus he deals with us as individuals. If we be without chastisement, then we are bastards, and not sons.

There is a story of four blind men who visited a menagerie, and because they could not see, were permitted to feel of the elephant. One felt of his tail, another of his side, the third of his leg, and the fourth of his ear. Afterward they were disputing among themselves in the effort to come to some agreement as to what the elephant was like. The one who felt of his side said he was like a great wall, while the one who felt of his tail said, "Oh, no! he is only like a large rope." The others disagreed with both of these, and also with each other, for the one who felt of his leg said the elephant was like the trunk of a tree, and the one whose hand had handled the elephant's ear, said that his impression was that the animal was a very peculiar one, more closely resembling a large leather bag than anything else he could think of.

Blinded by sin and limited by our little lives to the narrow span of these few years, and by our feeble intellects to a few of the many facts that underlie his purposes, it is thus we are compelled to touch God's mighty providences only at certain points, and our impressions may be varied, and all of them wrong.

We may criticize and condemn as unjust his deeds, until our own hearts are moulded and hardened into the image of all the evil we attribute to him. Far better is it that faith should grasp and hold the great truth that God is love, and then, instead of judging and condemning God because we cannot now see the perfect symmetry of Love's ideal, we will wait for the future, when we shall know as we are known. Yes, wait in perfect faith, that when the whole of God's great plan is seen, the love that permeated every part will be manifest.

And, waiting thus, faith sweeps back the horizon of our lives, till we, too, inhabit eternity with him, our citizenship over yonder, our life the eternal life which he has given; and then, reasoning on the darkest of his providences, either in the history of the world or in our own lives, and reasoning from the standpoint of our settled and abiding confidence in his love, we shall be surprised to see how many of the shadows even here will vanish; and how the warm sunshine of his living presence will illumine and glorify many a dark corner in our hearts, from which, till now, our unbelief has excluded him.[1]

Notes:

1. For more on the subject of God's anger and the final end of sin and sinners, visit http://www.heavenlysanctuary.com and click on audio and video sermons on this topic.

XXII

The Plagues of Egypt

"Sing ye to the Lord, for he hath triumphed gloriously."

—Ex. 15:21

In the minds of many, another objection to the idea that God deals with his creatures only in love, is found in his terrible judgments upon Egypt, whereby his children were delivered from bondage.

It is admitted here that God loved his own people, the Israelites, and worked mightily for their deliverance; but it is thought that his dealings with the Egyptians were characterized only by unrestrained anger and wrath. Such fail to understand the meaning of those plagues, and also of the scripture which says:—

> "O give thanks unto the God of gods; for his mercy endureth forever. . . . To him that smote Egypt in their firstborn; for his mercy endureth forever; . . . and overthrew Pharaoh and his hosts in the Red Sea; for his mercy endureth forever. . . . To him which smote great kings; for his mercy endureth forever; and slew famous kings; for his mercy endureth forever."

It is evident that the psalmist in the contemplation of these very judgments of God, was impressed, not with his hatred and unrestrained anger, but rather with the wonderful endurance of his loving mercy. Such will be the attitude of our minds when we too are guided by the divine Spirit into that closer communion with the All-Truth, that shall make us also men after God's own heart.

What was God's purpose in the deliverance of Israel?—Not simply that they might be saved, but that through them he might so reveal himself to the world as to reach and save all who could be saved. The heart of the All-Father was then, as ever, yearning over all his children. All that he gave to Israel was "for us," and for all the Gentile world. The highest privilege of the Jewish people, had they attained to it by a faithful obedience, was simply to be the medium through which all nations should be blessed; and, indeed, in a certain sense, though not as it would have been, this will be realized in spite of their unbelief, for God's plan never fails because of our faithlessness.

The Egyptians once had a knowledge of the true God, the Creator, and so sacredly was he regarded that they refused to take his name upon their lips, but instead they called him the Sacred, the Self-existent, the Unnamable One. Although the Egyptians had gone the downward way from the worship of God to the worship of the sun, and from sun worship to star worship, and the lowest forms of nature worship, multiplying their gods till it became a proverb that there were more gods in Egypt than men, yet the knowledge of this true God still lingered as a shadowy belief, held by the elite, the educated few. These regarded the multitude of gods as only demigods, or lesser gods, yet they worshiped them instead of the supreme One, because they believed the devil's lie, that the Creator was too far above them and had too much to attend to, to notice their prayers or care for their worship.

When God sent Moses and Aaron to Pharaoh, he said from the burning bush, "Thus shalt thou say unto him, I AM THAT I AM hath sent me unto you;" that is, the Sacred, Self-existent, Unnamable One that you profess to believe in, hath sent me hither to demand that his people, the Israelites, shall be set free to go and worship him. Pharaoh said, "Who is the Lord, that I should obey his voice to let Israel go? I know not the Lord, neither will I let Israel go."

In this Pharaoh was partially honest. He did not believe that this supreme God cared for the worship of men, far less that he cared for the worship of those Hebrew slaves.

Paganism always ascribed its national success to the greatness of its guardian gods. So to Pharaoh it seemed that if the Israelites had a God at all, he was only the God of slaves, and under the control of their gods, sustaining about the same relation to them that the Hebrew people did to the Egyptians. For them, while in slavery to the Egyptians, to claim that their God was the God whom even he admitted to be above all, was preposterous; it was more, it was blasphemy against the gods of Egypt, and, worse than that, it was an assertion of their power, and a demand for their right of independence from the Egyptian yoke. What wonder that Pharaoh increased their burdens and applied the lash, thinking to whip such foolishness out of them! For him, the king of Egypt, to admit the claim of these slaves that their God, the God who demanded their freedom, was identical with the supreme God of gods, whom he regarded as above noticing even him, was for him to admit their right and power of independence, and their superiority as a race in the estimation of God, to even what he claimed for the Egyptians. What wonder that the haughty monarch refused to admit all this!

But every act of God in his dealing with him from this on was for the purpose of bringing him to see and admit this truth; and not only him, but the world through him. Had Pharaoh remained true to himself and the light that God revealed to him, he might have lost some slaves, but he would have found a loving Father, where before he had only in a theoretical way believed in a stern, immovable, uncaring, and unnoticing God. He is not the only one, however, who, when called upon to decide between things seen and things unseen, the temporal and the eternal, has decided wrong.

The very first sign that Moses was to give Pharaoh had a wonderful meaning. Moses cast down his rod, and it became a serpent. The magicians did likewise, or rather by magic made it appear to the people that they did likewise. But the serpent that came from Moses' rod devoured the other serpents, and then turned to a rod again in his hand.

The serpent in Egypt was held as sacred, and worshiped as a god. To deify reptiles and worship them is one of the lowest forms of idolatry, the last step in the downward way. These reptiles, since the serpent tempted Eve, have symbolized Satan, and their worship was devil worship inspired by fear. By this act, wrought in the power of God and according to his special direction, Moses demonstrated to Pharaoh that the God of the Hebrew slaves could make and unmake the Egyptian gods at his pleasure. He could create them and he could destroy them, and therefore he must be the God whom even he admitted to be above all, the only one who had the power to triumph over the very evil which they personified thus and worshiped through fear. In this there was not only a revelation of the true God, but also a proclamation of the gospel,—a revelation of the power to triumph over sin. Pharaoh saw the truth, but through pride and worldliness he refused to heed it, and thus his heart was hardened.

There is an old and true proverb that says, "Egypt is the gift of the Nile." Upon the annual overflow of this river depended the wonderful fertility of the soil, which would otherwise have been like the great Sahara, utterly incapable of supporting life. The Egyptians, recognizing this fact, instead of giving glory to God, personified and worshiped the river. They drank of its waters with reverence, believing they had power to heal disease and impart new life. Upon its banks was a magnificent temple, where was enshrined a colossal statue of this god Nilus, and to this the king and all the nobles resorted at fixed times for worship.

The God of the Hebrew slaves turned this river into blood, making it death-dealing instead of life-giving. The Egyptians could not drink of the water, for it stank; and not all the combined powers of the gods of Egypt could restore the river to its former state. The God of the Hebrews alone could restore the river, thus proving that to him alone was due all the reverence and worship which they had foolishly given to his work.

The frog also was a sacred animal, and was worshiped with much pomp by the Egyptians. The God of the Hebrew slaves multiplied the frogs till they became a terrible pest, and the land stank. The proud Pharaoh had to appeal to the God of his slaves, that the gods of Egypt, that had been made by him, might also be destroyed by him, for there was no power in all the deities of Egypt to effect this much-desired result. Still Pharoah resisted the truth and hardened his heart.

By the decree of this same omnipotent God of the Hebrew slaves, the very dust of Egypt became lice upon all men throughout the land. Now the louse was considered unclean. If it touched the person, it necessitated, among the Egyptians, as later among the Jews, a long process of purification before the priest could officiate at the altar, or the devout citizen appear there acceptably to offer sacrifice. Thus by the decree of Jehovah every temple of Egypt was closed, and every shrine was for a time deserted. There was no priest to officiate and no worshiper to offer sacrifice; and thus was it proved that the whole of that false system of worship, with its many temples and its multitudes of priests and priestesses, and its magnificent ceremonials, existed but by the sufferance of the supreme One, who in his tender mercy was seeking to lead all to him.

In Egypt there was one deity whose special duty it was to protect the land from the swarms of flies and destructive insects which sometimes infested it; and another, to whose worship was attributed the salubrious[1] climate and the absence of destructive storms. In spite of these deities, and notwithstanding every effort was made to propitiate them, at the command of the Hebrews' God the flies came in swarms with their poisonous sting, making life itself a burden; and at the same command the lightnings flashed, and the thunder rolled along the ground, while the terrible hail destroyed the crops and killed both man and beast found unprotected in the fields. The murrain[2] fell upon the cattle, killing even the sacred ox, the center of the abominable, lascivious Apis worship. The magnificent temple, the boast of Egyptian architecture, was deserted, or filled only with the silent mourners for the dead god. The silver trumpets of the priests and the songs of the nude dancing maidens were hushed.

What a revelation of the fact that there is one God, and one only! Not in all Egypt could there one honest, sincere soul still remain deceived by the hollow mockery of so vile a polytheism.

The worship of the sun was the very center and kernel of the state religion. In various forms, conceived of as possessing varied powers, he stood at the head of each different order of gods, and was personified as the god of gods. Yet at the command of the God who now demanded the freedom of the poor Hebrew slaves, the glory of this supposed supreme one vanished. He withdrew his shining, and in Egypt there was darkness that could be felt; but in the land of Goshen, where the Creator of the sun was acknowledged supreme, there was light.

Even in the death of the firstborn, that his people might be delivered, had they not resisted the light unto perfect blindness, the Egyptians might have beheld revealed the divine Love that had not withheld his Firstborn, yea, his Only Begotten, but had consented unto his death that they might have deliverance from the power of death, unto everlasting life. Even this was not so difficult a thought for them, for the power of the original promise of the divine Son over the hearts of mankind was witnessed to still, even in their religion, by many legends wherein the literal sun was fabled to play the part of the Sun of Righteousness.

A greater condemnation of idolatry, and a grander revelation of the true God as the only omnipotent one worthy of worship, could not be conceived of by the human mind. Yet God in mercy condescended thus to speak the truth to the ancient nations, not to the Egyptians only, for the knowledge of Israel and of their wonderful deliverance by the power of their God spread through all the land till the fear of them and the dread of them fell upon all people. Notwithstanding this wonderful revelation of God's power, and of the fact that the supreme God does care for his children, so that there is no excuse for the worship of demi-gods, it might be said of the Egyptians, that "they repented not to give him glory."

Still there were some who did repent, for a mixed multitude of the Egyptians chose the part of the Israelites, and went up with them. What wonder that when delivered thus with such mighty power, and brought through the Red Sea on dry land,—what wonder that they sang a new song, a song of triumph, saying: "I will sing unto the Lord, for he hath triumphed gloriously. . . . The Lord is my strength and song, and he is become my salvation."

He who beholds these plagues in the true light, will see in them no conflict with the great truth that God is love; instead, he will see revealed therein a love that broods over us ever, though in trial and darkness, though in slavery and oppression; a love that, while seeking to bring us to freedom and joy in him, yea, even to the land of rest that floweth with milk and honey, seeks also so to reveal himself to all others that they too, through our deliverance, may find him their deliverer and their supreme joy.

Notes:

1. Favorable to or promoting health or well-being.
2. A pestilence or plague especially affecting domestic animals.

XXIII

The Seven Last Plagues

"He will plead with all flesh; he will give them that are wicked to the sword."

—Jer. 25:31

Those who have read carefully the preceding chapters will have discovered that the one thought which the author has endeavored to make prominent, is that whether in the refreshing dew and gently falling rain, or in storm and tempest; whether in the loving ministration of Jesus, or in the destruction of the world by a flood of waters,—whatever the *action* may be, the *motive* of God is love, for God is love.

The seven last plagues may appear to be an exception to this rule. To those who regard the closing of probation as an arbitrary act on the part of God, a willful shutting off of mercy because the set time for mercy is past, and who believe that the plagues are poured out after such closing of probation, this manifestation of wrath on the part of God must ever remain the great exception, the one act of God utterly unreconciled and unreconcilable with a motive of love. It is as though God said, "I will have mercy and accept repentance for a certain length of time, and after that I will not have mercy nor accept repentance. Moreover, after that time is past, and therefore after the sinner's case is hopeless and no experience of suffering can benefit him, then I will glut[1] my rage and revenge and pour out all my vials of torture upon his defenseless head." This is the pagan conception of God,—a being who is capable of all the passions of men, only greater and more terrible in his anger and revenge. God is the same yesterday, today, and forever. If this is his character when pouring out the plagues, it has ever been his character; Satan's representation of God has been the just one; and the pagan sacrifice of some innocent victim to propitiate the ever easily offended Deity was necessary,—in short, paganism is true.

How different the God revealed in Jesus Christ!—infinite and *eternal* in his mercy and love, taking no pleasure in the necessary death of the wicked, but ever, with every experience of both joy and sorrow, seeking to lead them through repentance to life. How different the closing of probation, when it is understood to be man's finally forsaking God, instead of God's forsaking man! How different the closing of the doors of the heavenly temple by sorrowing angels, who weep that the last sinner has finally refused repentance, from the shutting of those doors by an angry Deity, perhaps in the very face of those who may chance to be late!

It has been thought that the seven last plagues will be the result of the closing of Christ's intercession, so that nothing will intervene between the wrath of an offended God and the defenseless head of doomed man. This idea, when carried to this extreme, utterly separates between the Father and the Son; it denies the great truth so often asserted by Jesus, that he and his Father are one; that he is but the revelation, or manifestation, of the Father; that, as the poet says—

"The love that Jesus gave
Was still the Father's own;
Nor jealous claim of rivalry
Divides the cross and throne."

It is admitted by all that this wrath manifested in the plagues is "unmixed;" the wine is undiluted with water. But the wrath of God is revealed through Jesus to be his wrath against sin, because sin is the enemy of the sinner. It is, therefore, only another manifestation of his love. God can have no sympathy for sin, for to do so would put him into partnership with Satan, the enemy of all joy. But God does have infinite sympathy, or rather pity, for the sinner. This last manifestation of wrath must be unmixed, undiluted; that is, it must reveal to the world and the universe *just how* God hates sin, even a sin that the world has thought would pass unnoticed by him; nevertheless, the motive of God back of this wrath against sin may be, and is, infinite love to all his creatures.

A good father punishes his child for doing wrong, not only for the benefit of the child, but also for the benefit of the whole family. The punishment reveals his unmixed hatred for the *action*, not for the child himself. The restraining force of the lesson of that punishment upon the child and upon the family is just in proportion to the realization by the children of this fact. If they see that the father punishes in love, and for their good, and that the punishment grieves his tender heart more than theirs, they learn thereby to hate the evil act, and to love the tender parent. If the parent punishes in anger, they see thereby that he is no better than themselves, and their hearts cling to the sin, and learn to hate the one who punishes. This is why "our Father" has told us that he takes pleasure, not in the punishment, but in the repentance.

Now, the seven last plagues are a punishment of the All-Father upon his rebellious children. They are sent either in anger or in love, and their effect upon the universe of intelligent beings, and the effect of the belief in them upon our hearts now, will, as revealed in the above illustration, be in accord with our understanding of them. They may be to us a revelation of a God who, like ourselves, is capable of anger, hatred, and revenge, and therefore cannot reasonably condemn such passions in us; or they may become to us a revelation of a God of infinite love, who hates sin with an infinite hatred because it is the enemy of those he loves.

Almost the whole typology of the Bible depends upon the fact that the leading of the children of Israel out of Egypt, across the Red Sea, and into the land of Canaan, is a type of the leading of the true Israel out of the darkness of this world into the true Canaan of rest. The force of this type is recognized in the book of Revelation, where the redeemed on the sea of glass are represented as singing the song of Moses and the Lamb. The two songs are one; one is the type of the other. The children of Israel were delivered by a series of plagues through which God revealed himself to the Egyptians, and also revealed his hatred of the sin of idolatry. Those plagues were not sent to destroy the Egyptians meaninglessly, through a motive of wrath, but to reveal God to them, giving them one more, one last, chance to go with his people; and all this through the motive of love. God is to set his hand a second time to the deliverance of Israel. He will make a final revelation to the world of himself and of his hatred of sin.

John says, "I looked, and, behold, the temple of the tabernacle of the testimony in heaven was opened: and the seven angels came out of the temple, having the seven plagues, . . . and the temple *was filled with smoke from the glory of God, and from his power; and no man was able to enter into the temple,* TILL THE SEVEN PLAGUES OF THE SEVEN ANGELS WERE FULFILLED."In these words, the Lord definitely informs us just how the plagues stand related, in point of time, to the closing work in the heavenly sanctuary, and therefore to the closing of probation. This is the antitype; to understand it we must go back to the type.

When was the time, and the only time in the yearly round of the earthly ministration, when the temple was filled with smoke, and no man permitted to enter? Was it after the ministration was completed, and probation as typified by that year's ministration at an end? or was it during the closing moments of that ministration, while the high priest was in the most holy place? We answer, The last is the truth. The tenth day of the seventh month was the day of atonement. The high priest, however, did not really enter the most holy place to make the final atonement until the closing minutes of that day, just before sunset. During the day the assistant priests were in the temple, but when the climax was reached, the high priest went into the holy of holies alone; all other priests retired even from the outer apartment of the temple, the temple was filled with smoke, and no one was permitted to enter till the ministration was completed. (See Lev. 16:13, 17; also elsewhere.) This is the type; and Rev. 15:8 is the antitype.

Since the termination of the prophetic periods, in 1844, we have been in the day of atonement, but the assistant priests have been in the temple above, and the ministration has been going on in the outer apartment as well. When the hour of the atonement arrives, all will retire, Jesus will enter the holy of holies alone, and at that time, not after he comes out and the door is shut, will the plagues be poured out.

With this statement, every text in the Scriptures that relates at all to the closing of probation is in perfect agreement, while they are all in direct antagonism to the idea that probation closes before the plagues begin to fall. It must be remembered, however, that when we speak of the closing of probation, we mean, not the closing of probation for some individuals, but the complete closing of probation for the world. This distinction is all-important, for we have seen that the marking and sealing work, or the closing of probation, is progressive, and covers a period of time. The plagues fall upon those who have the mark of the beast, that is, upon *those persons whose probation is closed,* because they have fully committed themselves to the powers of evil.

But while they fall upon *individuals* whose probation is closed, they fall before the probation of all the world is closed, that is, before all have taken the final step that commits them wholly to evil. They fall for the purpose of so revealing God's truth and his wrath against sin, as to help those who are deciding, to decide aright.

Satan, the Bible says, will be working with all power and signs, and lying wonders, and with all deceivableness of unrighteousness, so that, if it were possible, he would deceive the very elect. Under these circumstances, if God wrought only with the silent power of the truth, some honest souls, whose intellects have not been trained to quickly recognize and appreciate the truth, might be deceived. God will not permit this. He will set his hand a second time to deliver his people. He will manifest himself openly and mightily, as of old.

The Son of God, the divine Word, will be in the temple during the plagues, for after the pouring out of the seventh vial his voice is heard *out of the temple from the throne*, that is, from the inner apartment of the heavenly sanctuary, saying "It is done."[2]

After the sixth plague is poured out, this solemn warning is given, "Behold, I come as a thief. Blessed is he that watcheth, and keepeth his garments, *lest he walk naked, and they see his shame*." All will admit that this is speaking of the garments of divine righteousness, with which the redeemed will be clothed.

Then there is danger that this garment may be lost at that time, else why this solemn warning? But if the garment of righteousness can be lost after six plagues have been poured out, then it can also be gained; for at the same time that the Lord says, "He that is righteous, let him be righteous still," he says also, "He that is filthy, let him be filthy still." Therefore *probation is not closed after the sixth plague is poured out.*

"And he gathereth them into a place called in the Hebrew tongue Armageddon."[3] It is under this plague that the wicked are gathered for the great battle. Joel describes this same gathering thus: "Assemble yourselves, and come, all ye heathen, and gather yourselves together round about: thither cause thy mighty ones to come down, O Lord. Let the heathen be wakened, and come up to the valley of Jehoshaphat: for there will I sit to judge all the heathen round about. Put ye in the sickle, for the harvest is ripe: come, get you down; for the press is full, the fats overflow; for their wickedness is great. Multitudes, multitudes *in the valley of decision:* for the day of the Lord is near in the valley of decision." Here it is seen that when they are gathered here, under the sixth plague, instead of their cases all having been decided long before, they are right now in the valley of decision, where they must make their choice at once. How appropriate, then, the warning to watch, lest the heavenly garment be lost.

The prophet Zephaniah, speaking of this gathering of the wicked who are without shame, or, as one translator puts it, without desire of repentance, says: "Gather yourselves together, yea, gather together, O nation not desired; *before the decree bring forth, before the day pass as the chaff*, before the fierce anger of the Lord come upon you, before the day of the Lord's anger come upon you." Then he speaks of the righteous with an admonition much like that in Revelation about the garments of righteousness: "Seek ye the Lord, all ye meek of the earth, which have wrought his judgment; seek righteousness, seek meekness: it may be ye shall be hid in the day of the Lord's anger." Here this gathering, which is under the sixth plague, is plainly declared to be *before the decree bring forth, before the day pass as the chaff,* as it is before the fierce anger of the Lord against sin, which under the seventh plague destroys the unrepentant sinner from the earth.

The drying up of the river Euphrates under the sixth plague is the coming to his end of the Turkish power as described by the prophet Daniel in the last verse of the eleventh chapter. But it is *at that time* that Michael, or Christ, shall "stand up," or lay aside his priestly garments, and take his kingly robe; and then will come the climax of the time of trouble under the seventh plague, which is the one universal plague, and the one which sums up in itself all the others.[4]

How perfectly this agrees with the prophet John's picture in Revelation, where, after the destruction of the Turkish power under the sixth plague, the Son of God is represented under the seventh plague as stepping forth from the temple, saying, "It is done," while there are lightnings, and thunderings, and an earthquake, and great hail, and the fierceness of divine wrath against sin, destroying the world.

Again and again the prophets speak of the Lord in these plagues as "*pleading with all flesh*," and giving them that are wicked to the sword.[5] This reveals God's motive, not to needlessly torture those who are past hope, but so to reveal his truth and manifest his wrath against sin, as to help those who are still in the valley of decision to decide aright.

As it was in Egypt, so here, there will be just two classes. The little, despised company will be looking for Jesus to come and set up his kingdom. All others, led away by the great delusion, will be looking for that kingdom to come in some way through the gateway of politics. The whole world will be looking for a theocracy. Satan will be working in mighty power, showing miracles, so that, if possible, he may deceive the very elect. God's truth will have been proclaimed to the world with power, yet if God showed no outward manifestation of power to offset Satan's miracles, some might be honestly deceived.

As in the deliverance of ancient Israel, every plague drew the line between the proud and haughty Egyptians and their false system of idolatry on the one hand, and the despised slaves, who were worshipers of the true God, on the other, showing that the God of gods was with the despised few; so here, the noisome sore may fall upon those who have the mark of the beast, but no plague shall come nigh the dwelling of those who have made God their refuge, and his truth their shield and buckler.

The multitudes who are looking for the false christ and accepting the false theocracy may have blood to drink; but of that little company it is said, "Bread shall be given him; his water shall be sure." The sun may scorch its worshipers with great heat, but "he that dwelleth in the secret place of the Most High shall *abide under the shadow* of the Almighty." Again and again, when a plague is poured out, it is said of the wicked world, "They repented not to give him glory;" "They repented not of their deeds." This plainly shows that the time for repentance was not arbitrarily closed. It shows that the plagues were given by a merciful, loving Father, to lead men to repentance; but they, hardened by sin, would not heed the lesson.

The Egyptians did not repent, but went on to destruction in the Red Sea. Yet some of them repented. A mixed multitude went up with Israel to the promised land. So here God may have some fruit of his loving labor; some may repent, but of the world it is true, "They repented not." Nevertheless, not until the seventh plague is poured out and there are voices and thunders and lightnings and a great earthquake,—not until then is Christ's voice heard saying, "It is done."

What is done? The plan of redemption will not be complete for more than a thousand years yet. Oh, this is God saying in infinite mercy, and grief of wounded love, as Jesus spake when he wept over Jerusalem, and pronounced its doom,—it is God saying, "I have done my last and utmost for the human soul. I sent prophet after prophet, and some they stoned, and some they put to death. I sent my only Son, but him they slew. From the very seat of infinite mercy,—from out the door of the still open temple, I sent these seven angels to reveal my unmixed hatred and wrath against sin, that men might take final warning, and turn to me; but they would not. I have done my last and utmost, and still they repent not. *It is done.* He that is filthy will be filthy still, and he that is righteous will be righteous still."

Then the Saviour comes out, and the temple is closed, for there will be no more applications for mercy. In a little while he puts on his kingly robes, and comes to take his own eternally to himself, and with the knife of love to cut out forever from the universe the cancer of sin, that righteousness and joy may reign supreme forever. O, this is a lesson to all God's creatures, of his hatred for sin, and also of his love for sinners. This is love, for "God is love."[6]

Notes:

1. To fill to satiety.
2. Rev. 16:17.
3. Rev. 16.16.
4. Dan. 11:45; 12:1.
5. Jer. 25:31; Isa 66:16.
6. Ellen White makes the following comment which is appreciated by the publishers: "I was shown that the judgments of God would not come directly out from the Lord upon them, but in this way: They place themselves beyond His protection. He warns, corrects, reproves, and points out the only path of safety; then if those who have been the objects of His special care will follow their own course independent of the Spirit of God, after repeated warnings, if they choose their own way, then He does not commission His angels to prevent Satan's decided attacks upon them. It is Satan's power that is at work at sea and on land, bringing calamity and distress, and sweeping off multitudes to make sure of his prey. And storm and tempest both by sea and land will be, for Satan has come down in great wrath. He is at work. He knows his time is short and, if he is not restrained, we shall see more terrible manifestations of his power than we have ever dreamed of." Manuscript Releases, Vol. 14, 3.1.

XXIV

The Second Resurrection

"Ye are my witnesses, saith the Lord, that I am God."

—Isa. 43:12

The plagues, in which is to be poured out God's unmixed wrath against sin, still come from a heart filled with pitying love for the sinner. God takes no pleasure in the misery of the wicked, but only longs for them to turn and repent. It is only after the last plague is poured out, and they still remain impenitent, that he is compelled to say, "It is done;" "he that is filthy, let him be filthy still." This is but an announcement of the fact that the last impenitent soul has sinned beyond repentance, and therefore beyond pardon.

By this it is not meant that the probation of no one closes until that time. The probation of many has doubtless closed already, and it is probable that the probation of a large majority of the wicked will close before the plagues are poured out. It should be remembered that the sealing of the wicked for Satan, as the sealing of the righteous for God, is an individual work, and a progressive work. It is not the turning away of God from the soul, but the hardening of the soul against God. The sealing, or marking, is complete, and therefore probation ends for the individual when that heart becomes so hardened in sin as to turn away from God's loving power as revealed in his everlasting gospel, and pronounce it all the work of Satan. It is doubtless true that some have gone thus far already. It is certain that as the truth goes with power, many will continue to resist and reject it.

The probation of the world, as a world, however, is only closed when the last sinner has taken this stand, and God has solemnly announced the fact in the awful, "It is done;" "he that is filthy, let him be filthy still." Not until this time is the world given over by God's lingering love; and to the writer it seems absolutely positive from the Bible that this is not before the pouring out of the plagues, but just after the seventh plague is poured out. This being so, the plagues are not an illustration of a wrath that delights in hopeless and useless torture, but of a love that lingers long in its sublime and godlike effort to turn the sinner into the right way. It is true the plagues reveal God's unmingled wrath to the universe, but it is unmingled wrath and hatred for sin, because of unmingled, pitying love for the sinner whom the sin is destroying. This is the God whom Jesus revealed in his whole life,—a God who hates the sin because he loves the sinner. This is the God *who is one with that Saviour* in all the love he manifested on this earth, and who is, with him, the same yesterday, today, and forever. He it is with whom there is no past and no future, for he inhabiteth eternity,—he, the all-unchanging, the all-embracing, the all-satisfying Love.

But it will be asked, If this is God, if he has no desire to torture or to punish for the sake of the punishment itself, why are the wicked resurrected to suffer the second death? Why, when once in their graves, are they not left there forever? To the thoughtful mind that has carefully considered all the points of the preceding chapters, this is not a difficult question. It is true, however, that the greatest truth lies closest to the most dangerous error, even as the most ravishing harmony is that which lies nearest to discord. For this reason, many are too timid to think to the line and get the truth. To do this requires the courage that comes from a consciousness of divine guidance,—a simple faith that the Spirit, if trusted, will lead into all truth.

Now, the most dangerous error is to trust to a future probation. To do this is to procrastinate without excuse, since God closes this probationary period with the positive announcement that the filthy will be filthy still.

But why will there be no future probation?—Not because God is not good enough to continue man's probation indefinitely, if there would be any use in such a continuation; but because God has done his utmost here in infinite love to turn the soul to him, and the soul that has resisted it here, and even pronounced the work wrought by the power of that love but the work of Satan,—*God knows* that soul would resist it ever and always.

I say that God knows this, but it must also be revealed to the world, and to the universe, so that they may see and know; else they cannot, at the destruction of the wicked, of their own free will, join in the spontaneous song of universal praise, ascribing to him justice and truth in all his ways. That the universe of intelligent beings may see this, and so be prepared to join in that song, thus being united in love to God as one family in heaven and in earth, and so preventing all danger of future sin,—this is the meaning of the second resurrection.

The belief in a future probation, which is becoming so prevalent today, rests upon a *true idea* of the character of God; but also upon a false idea of the effect of sin upon the human heart, and therefore a *false idea* of the nature of the closing of probation. One of the premises is true, the other is false; hence, according to the law of syllogisms, the conclusion, which is that there must be a future probation, is false also. The reason given is that God is too good ever to cut off the truly repenting soul from the privilege of pardon and peace. This is emphatically true, but it does not follow, as believers in this theory think, that there will be a future probation. And why not?—Simply because (and this is what they do not see), *if God is so good,* SIN IS SO BAD that, persisted in, it hardens the soul beyond the power of repentance, yea, beyond the reach of the Holy Spirit to lead it to repentance. And this point is reached before probation is closed here; hence there is absolutely no use in a future probation, as no one would improve it to repent. Not only is it true that there is no use in a future probation, but there is absolutely no possibility of such probation. If God had arbitrarily cut off probation here, he could, and being a loving Father, he would have given man another chance. But God has cut off no one. Man has rejected God. God could not, therefore, give another probation without interfering with the free will of man, thus destroying character.

How does God propose to reveal this great fact to the universe, so that in all the future, after the wicked are destroyed and redemption is complete, there will never be one intelligent being who will ever be tempted even to think that if probation had continued a little longer, or God had done a little more, others might have been led to repentance? Ah! this is how: All those who have died will be raised from their graves. Among the mighty hosts of the resurrected wicked there will be many who died suddenly. Not realizing the watchfulness of a Providence without whom not a sparrow falleth, far less any human soul, till the Father sees he has made his final choice, we might say of this one or that, "If he had had a little longer time, he would have repented." So now here he is, alive again, and the Father's mercy and love are still the same.—"from everlasting to everlasting." It may be said that probation is at an end, and this is true; but here will be revealed the fact that God never closed the probation of any man; the man closed it himself by rejecting God. If probation is at an end, it is not that God is changed,—not that he is less ready to receive repentance, but that, as he has announced, the last man has finally refused to give repentance. Here this fact is held up before the universe.

Of all the hosts of the resurrected wicked, not one manifests any genuine sorrow for sin. The city of the redeemed is there before them, in its matchless splendor, revealing the love of God that they have slighted. The outlying camp of the saints shows beforehand a sample of the redeemed world, from which every trace of sin is removed. All this holds out, in vivid contrast to their miserable condition, all that God in love has longed to do for them, and yet there is no true repentance. They see Abraham, Isaac, and Jacob in the kingdom of God, and they themselves shut out, not by any arbitrary decree of God, but by their own refusal to enter by the appointed way. Before the universe they prove themselves to be indeed thieves and robbers, by seeking to climb up some other way. If they long for the external glories of the city of the redeemed, they do not long for the internal glories of the Christly life, of which these external glories are but a result and a reflection, and without which they are impossible. They are maddened by the sight of the glory and joy of which they themselves *are incapable.*

Every one of the mighty multitude joins hands with the prince of darkness, and takes up arms against the kingdom of everlasting love. Here, as on the cross of Calvary, is revealed the fact that persistent sin, in the heart of every sinner, would never be satisfied till it dethroned God and reigned in his stead. Untouched and untendered by that life and death of love, sin is the same here as when it mocked at the foot of the cross. If the fire comes down and destroys the wicked, it is only when every intelligent being in the universe can see that this is the only way that the government of love, which only makes joy possible, can be continued and perpetuated.

Every sinner that is destroyed is taken with the weapons in his hand with which, if possible, he would dethrone God and murder his children. Satan, leading his mighty armies, advances. They go up on the breadth of the earth, and encompass the camp of the saints about, and the beloved city. It is then that fire comes down and destroys them. Their final destruction is the final deliverance of all the righteous. Is it any wonder that the universe, looking on, says with one universal song of praise, "Great and marvelous are thy works, Lord God Almighty; just and true are thy ways, thou King of saints"? Is it any wonder that intelligent beings, beholding this mighty contrast of sin and its dark results, with righteousness and its attendant joy, shall learn to hate sin and love righteousness, till all danger of sin, in all worlds, shall be overpast? For, saith the Lord, "Affliction shall not rise up a second time."

In concluding these chapters, the author would express his overpowering sense of the weakness and incapacity of the human mind to comprehend, and of human language to reveal, the wisdom which is unsearchable, and the love which passeth knowledge. There are many who are troubled with constant doubts of God's love for them, and of their acceptance with him. They fail to see Love's hand in God's dealings with the world, and, worse still, they fail to see this hand in his dealings with them in their own lives. It may be that their path has been overshadowed with darkness, and they have walked wearily and despondingly. If to some such these words may come as an evangel of peace, revealing the great truth that God's love is eternal and unchanging, rising above and reaching beyond our unworthiness and our sin,—the one unchangeable thing in a world of fickleness and change; and if this consciousness may thus come to abide with them till they know that he is not far from them in any moment of trial and need, but that instead he is *in them and through them and above them all,* their refuge and strength,—ah, if this consciousness may come to them, till they rest quietly and trustingly and joyfully in the Everlasting Arms, the author will be satisfied, and to Christ be all the praise.

Appendix

It should be remembered that it is only under the seventh plague, or rather, the culmination of all six in the seventh, that we are told that "great Babylon came in remembrance before God, to give unto her the cup of the wine of the fierceness of his wrath." Rev. 16:19. This is after Christ has left the temple, as described in verse 17. It could not have taken place before; for this unmixed wrath sweeps the wicked from the earth, and it is not in God's character to destroy a man while there is a possible chance that he will repent. At the time of the pouring out of this fierceness of his wrath, the message has been given, and Christ has declared, "It is done."

"When the third angel's message closes, mercy no longer pleads for the guilty inhabitants of earth. The people of God have accomplished their work. They have received 'the latter rain,' 'the refreshing from the presence of the Lord,' and are prepared for the trying hour before them. Angels are hastening to and fro in heaven. An angel returning from the earth announces that his work is done; the final test has been brought up on the world, and all who have proved themselves loyal to the divine precepts have received 'the seal of the living God.' Then Jesus ceases his intercession in the sanctuary above. He lifts his hands, and with a loud voice says, '*It is done!*' and all the angelic host lay off their crowns as he makes the solemn announcement: 'He that is unjust, let him be unjust still; and he which is filthy, let him be filthy still; and he that is righteous, let him be righteous still; and he that is holy, let him be holy still.' "—*Great Controversy*, p. 613.

Here it is plainly seen that the closing of the third message, the closing of the sealing work, and therefore the closing of the world's probation, is definitely located under the pouring out of the seventh plague, when Christ steps out from the temple saying, "It is done."

The "It is done" of the seventh plague, and the "He that is filthy, let him be filthy still," are immediately associated together. This is also done in "Early Writings," chapter entitled, "Third Message Closed," p. 140, where we read as follows: "Then I saw Jesus, who had been ministering before the ark containing the ten commandments, throw down the censer. He raised his hands, and with a loud voice said, 'It is done.' And all the angelic host laid off their crowns as Jesus made the solemn declaration, 'He that is unjust, let him be unjust still, etc.'"

It will be seen that this involves all that has been presented in this volume concerning the close of probation, namely, that while the probation of individuals is closing, perhaps even now, all have not made their choice, and therefore the world's probation will not close until Jesus, in the beginning of the seventh plague, leaves the temple saying, "It is done."

The expression, "It was impossible for the plagues to be poured out while Jesus officiated in the sanctuary," which closely follows the last quotation in "Early Writings," must be understood to mean the plagues in their fullness, culminating in the seventh. Understood in any other way, it is a contradiction of the proceeding quotations, as well as of the plain testimony of Scripture; but understood thus, all is harmony. It was thus that Daniel said, "I was astonished at the vision, but none understood it," yet all but one symbol had been explained and understood.

This climax of the plagues under the seventh is plainly declared to occur after the angel with the seal returns from earth to heaven, announcing that his work is done. ("*Great Controversy*," p. 613.)

But the six men, or six angels, with slaughter weapons in their hands, were to follow the man with the writer's inkhorn, or the angel with the seal, and strike those upon whom he did not set his seal, *as he proceeded with his work*. (See Eze. 9; also Testimony No. 31, p. 203-209.) Thus we see that while the six men, or six angels, do not strike a single person until the